Twayne's English Authors Series

EDITOR OF THE VOLUME

Kinley E. Roby

Northeastern University

Peter Shaffer

TEAS 261

PETER SHAFFER

By DENNIS A. KLEIN

University of South Dakota

TWAYNE PUBLISHERS

A DIVISION OF G. K. HALL & CO., BOSTON

Published in 1979 by Twayne Publishers,
A Division of G. K. Hall & Co.
All Rights Reserved

Printed on permanent/durable acid-free paper and bound
in the United States of America

First Printing

Frontispiece photograph of
Peter Shaffer

Library of Congress Cataloging in Publication Data

Klein, Dennis A
Peter Shaffer

(Twayne's English authors series ; TEAS 261)
Bibliography: p. 155–61
Includes index.
1.   Shaffer, Peter, 1926 -
—Criticism and interpretation.
PR6037.H23Z7   822'.9'14   78-31239
ISBN 0-8057-6738-X

For my family
in loving memory
of
my father

Contents

About the Author

Dennis A. Klein received the Doctor of Philosophy degree with a specialization in modern Spanish drama from the University of Massachusetts in 1973. Previous to writing the present book, Dr. Klein's major publications were all on the Spanish playwright Federico García Lorca. He is a regular contributor to the *García Lorca Review* and *Hispania,* for which he is a book reviewer and the indexer. Dr. Klein is also a member of the committee which compiles the *International Bibliography* for the Modern Language Association. He is co-author and a member of the editorial board for a two-volume, annotated bibliography on García Lorca. The author is presently an Associate Professor of Spanish at the University of South Dakota.

Preface

The scope of Peter Shaffer's theater is vast. It ranges from the hilarious antics of *Black Comedy* to the psychological tension of *Equus*, from the domestic tragedy of *Five Finger Exercise* to the historical spectacle of *The Royal Hunt of the Sun*, and in a *corpus* of only ten works it encompasses everything from the stark drama of *Shrivings* to the broad farce of *The Public Eye* and misses little in between. Shaffer's plays include the sprawling epic of the Spanish conquest of the New World and the comedy of the traditional European farce; the plots are as time-honored as the conflict between an old, lackluster husband married to a spirited young wife, and as timely as the Peace Movement. Shaffer probes questions as intimate as identity crises and sexual self-doubt and as far-reaching as loneliness and man's need for worship.

As a dramatist, Mr. Shaffer has no social ax to grind. He does not write didactic plays of social criticism or protest, but rather he writes about people in conflict with themselves: a young man preoccupied with preserving his individuality; a conquering hero obsessed with eternalizing his name; a young wife living with a husband who does not understand her; a guilt-ridden alcoholic agonizing with his conscience. And his plays are about people in conflict with each other, by twos, by threes, by fours, and by whole cultures: husbands pitted against wives, fathers against sons, believers against skeptics, Christians against Incas. The characters are domineering and oppressed, religious and atheistic, self-confident and insecure, painfully honest and benignly false. They compete with each other for love, for power, for glory, or just for the satisfaction of proving that their view of the world is right. Shaffer's plays are as traditional in their structure as the weekend-cottage Naturalism of *Five Finger Exercise* and as contemporary as the overlapping dialogues of *Shrivings*. Shaffer uses techniques of game-playing and mistaken identity, light and darkness, music and mime, crystal balls and placebos. There are moments as tender as playing the love duet from *Madame Butterfly* and others as horrifying as blinding horses.

Analysis of Peter Shaffer's work is a problem for criticis because they cannot pigeon-hole him as belonging to a "school" or "movement." His drama defies the convenient labels of Theater of Anger, of Revolt, or of Absurdity. When Shaffer started writing for the London stage, his drama was theatrically anachronistic: while his contemporaries were producing "Angry" plays of social protest, he was concerning himself with the domestic problems of the middle class; while much of Europe was involved with the "Absurd," Shaffer was writing "well-made" plays in the tradition of Sir Terence Rattigan, in clear, precise prose. After Shaffer wrote *Five Finger Exercise*, he was afraid of being ·categorized as a writer of "week-end cottage naturalism." That need never have been a worry of his, because subsequently he went on to produce one of the most varied programs in any playwright's repertoire.

This study will focus on the characters, themes, and techniques as they develop throughout Shaffer's career as a writer. The organization of the book is basically chronological with the exception of *The Royal Hunt of the Sun*, which, for its characters and themes, is more logically grouped with *Shrivings* and *Equus* than treated between *The Public Eye* and *Black Comedy*. Each chapter begins with the stage record of the play under consideration. Then, for the benefit of the reader who is unfamiliar with Shaffer's plays, there is a substantial plot summary. Each chapter gives an analysis of the themes, techniques, and especially the characters as individuals, in contact with one another, and their relationship to other characters in Shaffer's plays. The chapters conclude with a critical appraisal of the plays, from the point of view of the reviewers as well as from that of the present writer.[1] The chapters on *Five Finger Exercise* and *Equus* are especially detailed because the first provides the key to understanding Peter Shaffer's dramaturgy, and the last is his most widely acclaimed success.

A minimum of space is devoted to the state of the British theater when Shaffer began his career as a playwright. What discussion there is occurs at the end of the chapter on *Five Finger Exercise*, Shaffer's first play to be presented on the British stage. Considerations of the twentieth-century theater in general are available in fuller form elsewhere.[2] There is also a deliberate effort not to duplicate material already included in other works of the Twayne Series.[3] There will be no attempt to "read" the playwright into any of his characters or to conclude that attitudes or situations in his plays are in any way autobiographical. To do so would be to fail to treat each work as its own artistic end. There can be no attempt yet to determine what Shaffer's influence will be on modern drama: he is in mid-career and enjoying the peak of his success.

DENNIS A. KLEIN

Acknowledgments

My first note of thanks must go to Mr. Peter Shaffer, for writing the plays that inspired this study; for his time and interest in meeting with me and verifying the biographical information in my first chapter; for affording me the opportunity to study the only extant copy of "The Salt Land," which is in his possession; for granting me permission to quote freely from his plays. There is perhaps no other artist of a more generous and humanitarian spirit.

I owe a debt of thanks to several individuals and organizations in London for helping to make my research easier and more pleasant: to Mr. Marc Berlin of London Management, Mr. Shaffer's representative in Great Britain; to Mrs. Molly O'Daly Woods, the playwright's former housekeeper; to the British Museum; and to the British Broadcasting Corporation. All were helpful in providing me with valuable information.

Likewise, I thank the New York Public Library, which makes scholarly research possible in the United States; the Public Library of Vermillion, South Dakota, and its former supervisor, Mr. Robert Precoda; and the State Library of South Dakota.

I must also thank my former colleagues at the University of Missouri - Rolla: Dr. W. Nicholas Knight, who encouraged me to write this book; and Dr. Larry Vonalt, for his help in locating bibliographical items and in interpreting the plays. Deep thanks go to Dr. Gerald Cohen for his intellectual suggestions, constant encouragement, interest, and friendship. And I cannot fail to mention Mrs. Daisy Mae Burton and Mrs. Dorothy Hargis of the interlibrary loan office.

In the same vein, I thank the staff of the library of the University of South Dakota, headed by Mr. Bob Carmack, and especially the research and interlibrary loan departments, supervised by Mr. Max Leget and served by Mr. John Evans and Mrs. Dorothy Iverson. Thanks are also in order to the Department of Modern Languages and the Student Financial Aid Office for providing the secretarial help of Miss Vicki Bulian and Miss Carol Palmer, whose efforts were indispensable in the preparation of the final manuscript.

Acknowledgments

I again thank Mr. Shaffer as well as his authorized representation at the Lantz Office, Inc., of New York for their permission to quote from *The Royal Hunt of the Sun, The Private Ear, The Public Eye, Black Comedy, White Lies,* and *The White Liars,* as well as for permission to reproduce Mr. Shaffer's photograph. I thank Samuel French, Inc., for permission to quote from *Five Finger Exercise* and Mr. Peter Shaffer and Atheneum Publishers for permission to quote from *Equus* and *Shrivings.*

My deepest thanks go to Dr. Brent Froberg, Chairman of the Department of Classics at the University of South Dakota, for his close friendship, sincere encouragement, scholarly advice, and meticulous proofreading. If any errors remain in the text, they are through my own oversights.

For their love and moral support, I thank the relatives and friends who have always stood behind me and encouraged me in my endeavors: my mother, Mrs. Bertha Klein; my uncle and aunt, Mr. and Mrs. Joseph Berman; and three very close friends, Mr. Howard Hoffman, Mr. Herbert Friedson, and Mr. David Moore.

Chronology

1926	May 15, born in Liverpool, England.
1950	Bachelor's degree from Cambridge University.
1951	British publication of *The Woman in the Wardrobe*.
1952	British publication of *How Doth the Little Crocodile?*
1955	November 8, "The Salt Land" produced by ITV. British publication of *Withered Murder*.
1956	American publication of *Withered Murder*.
1956	Literary critic for *Truth* magazine.
1957	
1957	September 14, "The Prodigal Father" aired on BBC radio's *Saturday Matinee*. November 21, "Balance of Terror" produced by BBC television. American publication of *How Doth the Little Crocodile?*
1958	January 27, "Balance of Terror" aired on American television. July 16, London premiere of *Five Finger Exercise*.
1959	December 2, New York opening of *Five Finger Exercise*.
1962	Music critic for *Time and Tide* magazine.
1962	May 10, London premiere of *The Private Ear* and *The Public Eye*.
1963	October 9, New York opening of *The Private Ear* and *The Public Eye*. December 17, London premiere of *The Merry Roosters' Panto*. Film script for William Golding's *Lord of the Flies*, with Peter Brook. The New York production of *The Establishment* includes a sketch written for the television series "That Was the Week That Was."
1964	July 6, the premiere of *The Royal Hunt of the Sun* at the Chichester Festival; December 8, London opening.
1965	July 27, Chichester premiere of *Black Comedy*. October 26, New York opening of *The Royal Hunt of the Sun*.
1967	February 12, New York opening of *Black Comedy* and *White Lies*.
1968	February 21, London premiere of *Black Comedy* and *The White Liars*.
1970	February 5, London premiere of *The Battle of Shrivings*.

December 24, *Five Finger Exercise* aired on BBC's "Play of the Month."

1972   Film script of *The Public Eye*, also called *Follow Me!*

1973   July 26, London premiere of *Equus*.

1974   October 24, New York opening of *Equus*. Publication of *Shrivings*.

1977   Film version of *Equus*.

CHAPTER 1

Biography: Early and Minor Works

I Biography

PETER Levin Shaffer was born in Liverpool, England on May 15, 1926, the son of Jewish parents, Jack and Reka Shaffer. His twin brother, Anthony, is the author of the prize-winning play *Sleuth*, and Brian, a younger brother, is a biophysicist. His father worked in real estate and was always able to maintain a comfortable home for his family. In 1936, the Shaffer family moved to London, and from 1936 through 1942 were moved all over England. When they settled in London in 1942, Peter was enrolled at St. Paul's School. From 1944 to 1947, Peter and Anthony were conscripted as coal miners in Kent and Yorkshire. After Peter fulfilled his obligation as a "Bevin Boy," he enrolled in Trinity College of Cambridge University on a scholarship and received his baccalaureate degree in history in 1950. During his years as a student, Shaffer edited a magazine at Cambridge and felt his first stirrings as a writer. Since employment in publishing was scarce in London, he decided to move to New York, but there, too, his possibilities for employment were limited, and he took a job as a salesman in Doubleday bookshops in mid-Manhattan. He was not happy forcing himself on potential customers for a sale, and so he left the bookstores to work in the acquisitions department of the New York Public Library. He remained at the library until 1954, and then, bored with a career that he did not think was benefiting him, he returned to London and accepted a position with the music publishing firm of Boosey and Hawks, where he remained until 1955. He left to become a literary critic for *Truth* magazine and subsequently became a music critic for *Time and Tide*.

Shaffer wrote three detective novels, the first alone and the other two in conjunction with his brother Anthony. In 1951 *The Woman in the Wardrobe*, the first of the three, was published in London un-

der the pseudonym of Peter Antony. It is the only novel that was
not subsequently published in the United States. Peter and Anthony
collaborated on *How Doth the Little Crocodile?*, which appeared
under Peter Antony for its 1952 British publication and with the
authors' real names for the 1957 American publication. Their second novel together was *Withered Murder,* which appeared in London in 1955 and in New York in 1956, this time with no
pseudonyms.

He also wrote three scripts for radio and television, the first of
which he completed in New York and took back to London with
him. It was called "The Salt Land"; Shaffer hoped it would be
produced on stage, but instead it was televised by the ITV. "The
Prodigal Father" was a radio play produced on the BBC program
"Saturday Matinee," and "Balance of Terror" was produced both
in England by the BBC and subsequently on "Studio One" in the
United States.

Satisfied by the success of "The Salt Land" and "The Prodigal
Father," Shaffer decided to dedicate himself to writing a play intended for the West End. On July 16, 1958, *Five Finger Exercise*
had its debut at the Comedy Theatre in London, and Peter Shaffer
had come into his own as a dramatist. The play was an immediate
success and won for Mr. Shaffer the Evening Standard Award for
the best new playwright of the season. It moved to New York in
1959, and on December 2 opened at the Music Box, this time winning the New York Drama Critics' Circle Award for the best foreign
play of the 1959 - 60 season.[1]

Throughout the 1960s, there was hardly a time when Shaffer's
work was not being presented in London or New York, or in both
cities simultaneously. After having enjoyed international success
with *Five Finger Exercise,* Shaffer brought to the London stage *The
Private Ear* and *The Public Eye,* a pair of one-act plays of high comedy, which opened at the Globe Theatre in 1962. The following
year was one which gave exposure to Shaffer's works in London and
New York, on stage as well as on the screen: in 1963, *The Private
Ear* and *The Public Eye* opened at the Morosco Theatre in New
York; a sketch that Shaffer wrote for the television series "That Was
the Week That Was" was included in the New York production of
The Establishment;[2] *The Merry Roosters' Panto* opened at
Wyndham's Theatre in London; and, along with Peter Brook,
Shaffer worked on the film script of William Golding's *Lord of the
Flies.* In December 1964, less than a year later, *The Royal Hunt of*

the Sun opened at the Chichester Festival. The play began a successful run at the ANTA Theatre in New York in October 1965. In the same year, Lord Olivier (then Sir Laurence), the director of the National Theatre, commissioned Shaffer to write a comedy for the 1965 repertoire, and the result was *Black Comedy*. For its opening in New York at the Ethel Barrymore Theatre in 1967, Shaffer wrote another one-acter as a "curtain-raiser," originally entitled "A Warning Game" and later changed to *White Lies*. *White Lies* was rewritten and presented in London as *The White Liars* at the Lyric Theatre in 1968, again paired with *Black Comedy*.

The success that Shaffer enjoyed in the 1960s was only a prelude to that of the 1970s, despite a less than successful production of *The Battle of Shrivings* in London in 1970. In 1972, the film version of *The Public Eye* appeared, for which Shaffer wrote the film script. In 1973, *Equus*, his most recent play, opened at the National Theatre in London and has since been presented with overwhelming success in virtually every corner of the globe, and has won for Mr. Shaffer the universal enthusiasm of the public and the praise of the critics. The Atheneum Press edition of *Equus* includes a revised version of his 1970 play, entitled *Shrivings*. He also wrote the screenplay for the 1977 film version of *Equus*.

Mr. Shaffer presently resides in New York.

II   *The Detective Novels*

Seven pieces of Shaffer's writings fall into the categories of early or minor works: three novels, three television or radio scripts, and one pantomime, the texts of some of which have not been published. A study of these works, however cursory, is a necessary preliminary to focusing on the works written for the National Theatre, the West End, and Broadway. The three novels, which represent the writer's earliest creative efforts, are clearly a cut above standard detective fare. The novels, however, when read after a study of the plays of Peter and Anthony Shaffer, only hint at the talents of the authors of *Equus* and *Sleuth*. All three novels are similar in their structure and need not be treated in detail.

The Woman in the Wardrobe, subtitled "a light-hearted detective story," is the earliest of the three novels, published in London in 1951. Upon leaving his house, Mr. Verity sees a man climbing out of a window and suspects that a crime has been committed at a guest house at an English seaside resort in Sussex. Mr. Maxwell, a blackmailer and all-around scoundrel, has been murdered, and the murderer could have been anyone who knew him. Supersleuth Verity, whose vocation it is to solve mysteries between tea and supper, sets out to solve this case in his usual ingenious manner. The detective conducts his interviews of the suspects and reveals that the murder was committed by a drug addict whom Maxwell was blackmailing. More important than the details of the plot, however, are the elements in the novel which appear throughout Shaffer's writing career. There are frequent references to history and to the Greco-Roman civilizations, both of which are dominant features which span Shaffer's writing career to date: Mr. Verity lives in a home which he calls "Persepolis," and his hobby is archaeology. In the solution of the crime, Verity cannot resist what he refers to as a "coup de théâtre" and he uses tricks which force the murderer to reveal his guilt. (Shaffer employs a similar device in his plays, written as much as twenty-five years later.) The reader learns little about Mr. Verity the man, except that he considers his father to be nothing and a man he never knew. (He claims that when he was a boy of ten, his mother fell in love with a carpenter, and that the neighbors put it down to "religious mania.")

How Doth the Little Crocodile?, the second novel, appeared in England in 1952 and in the United States in 1957. Like *The Woman in the Wardrobe*, it was published in England under the pseudonym Peter Antony, while the American edition bears the names Peter and Anthony Shaffer. This time the supposedly murdered man is Sir Livingstone, who was involved in an adulterous affair with Miss Lovelace. She is murdered, and the killer could be either of the two jealous women in the novel or any number of men who possessed motives. The trick this time is for the detective to reveal that Livingstone staged his own "murder" and then planted clues pointing to all possible suspects. The details of the plot are incidental to the significant themes—the game-playing among the characters, the many references to the classical world, and to the theater and actors—which are common to the larger study of Shaffer's writing. Sir and Lady Livingstone prefigure the kinds of husbands and wives who appear in almost all of Shaffer's plays.

Withered Murder is the third and last of the novels. It was published both in England (1955) and in the United States (1956) under the names A. and P. Shaffer, with no pseudonyms in either country. Once again the setting is in a boardinghouse, at a seaside resort on the south coast of England. A murder takes place, and the detective-hero pledges to resolve it in one evening's time, and so he does. The list of suspects includes a spinster, two giddy maids, a professor from Germany, a minister and his wife, and an artist, all of whom possessed opportunity, means, and/or motive to commit the crime. Like the other two novels, there are the now-familiar allusions to the classical world, amorous triangles, and the theater; in addition, this time there is a defense of sadism from the mouth of the hero, as well as details which suggest lesbianism.

The three novels share more than bonds of just plot or classical references: there is a strong resemblance in their structure and style. In all of the novels, the body of the book (between the incidence of the crime and its solution) consists primarily of dialogue, much like a play, with the detective questioning his suspects one by one. They are the work of playwrights more than of novelists.

III   *Radio and Television Scripts*

Shaffer wrote three scripts for radio and television, one of which is no longer extant. "The Salt Land," which Shaffer wrote while he lived in New York, was aired by ITV on November 8, 1955.. Shaffer wrote the work for the theater and describes it as a "tragedy [constructed] along loosely classical lines, not for the sake of experiment, though experiment has its own fascination, but because the subject of Israel and immigration is truly heroic, and deserves classical treatment."[3]

"The Salt Land" represents Shaffer's first attempt at writing drama and is a beautiful work, rich in the elements that appear in his later plays. Since the only copy of the script is in Mr. Shaffer's possession, a detailed plot summary is in order. "The Salt Land" is a drama in two acts and five scenes.

The first scene takes place on the stern of a small boat which is bringing illegal immigrants into Palestine, in the fall of 1947. As the curtain rises, there is the sound of chanting from the Friday-evening Jewish Service for the Sabbath. Saul, the twenty-two-year-old captain of the vessel, is furious because the singing will attract the attention of a patrol ship, attention which he is trying to avoid. Saul belongs to a group called the Palmach, whose mission it is to help Jews escape from Europe. A conflict arises between two brothers, Arieh and Jo Mayer. Arieh, aged twenty-seven, is dressed in traditional, Orthodox garb and believes that the Jews should sit and wait, and that they will be delivered to the Promised Land when the Lord sees fit. Jo, five years his junior, wears contemporary clothes, smokes on the Sabbath, and has little tolerance for the Talmud, his brother, or the pacifist philosophy. Mr. Mayer, the father, stands in awe of his elder son but agrees with Jo that Jews have a right to their own land, as do all other men. Kulli, a young woman, sides with Arieh, and Jo says that a man like Arieh could easily kill her. Jo has lived in Paris and feels superior to his father and brother, who have spent their whole lives in the ghetto. He considers Arieh a man still living in the Middle Ages, whose knowledge is limited to the sacred names of God and the recipe for incense burned in the Temple; he has no practical knowledge to bring to Palestine. Mr. Mayer thinks Jo's life is all dishonesty, tricks, lies, and the most abject materialism—Jo has been active on the black market, for which he has spent time in prison. Jo does not think that his activities are any of his father's business and that his father should be happy that Jo, through his connections, was able to get him on the boat. Max Galinsky, another passenger, becomes filled with the thought of arriving in the Land and of living on a *kibbutz*, a venture the success of which Mr. Mayer doubts; he fears that people will tire of the communal life and will want their own homes. As Max cries because something may prevent their entering Palestine, the first scene ends.

Scene two takes place the next night. Jo is with his friend Mr. Mordecai, whose whole manner indicates a Frenchified, German businessman, dressed in the most corrupt, worldly style. They both believe that this trip was paid for with money and that prayers had nothing to do with it. Mordecai has placed himself on a superior level to the rest of the Jews, whom he thinks of as masochists who *like* suffering and being exiles. He made his money from the Nazis and by selling passports on the black market; now he is going to Palestine to milk it for all it is worth, and Kulli is appalled. Jo is to be his partner and translator. Arieh fears that the Jewish people have abandoned the Lord, and as a result will have to inhabit a wilderness, a salt land. The captain announces that the boat is now off the coast of Palestine and that the passengers should prepare to disembark.

The third scene takes place at the command post of a settlement in the Negev, in early October 1948: a sunlit scene of destruction. Arieh is the commander of a post, seriously deficient in arms and in men. He accepted the position after he heard the Voice, and he knew that the sword could be used for good purposes. Jo, who is sar-

castic regarding his brother's position in Palestine, has come to offer
Arieh tanks, trucks, and jeeps in return for a favor he will want later
when his brother has a high position in the state. Kulli begs Arieh to
have nothing to do with Jo or his deals. Arieh cannot lose the
chance of turning Palestine into Paradise and he decides to accept
Jo's offer. If need be, Arieh will break his word to Jo later, but he
must have the weapons now. He believes (or tells himself) that Jo
was sent to him by the Lord: in the fight for Israel, even the most
vile must serve.

Act Two, scene one, a Saturday morning in late summer 1949.
The scene is the communal room of a desolate settlement in the
Negev. Kulli is married to Arieh, whose father is offended that work
goes on, even on the Sabbath. Between acts, Jo was tried for
profiteering—making money out of the homeless—but was ac-
quitted for lack of witnesses willing to testify against him and
thereby incriminate themselves as accessories. Arieh's attitude has
changed: he will not order people to go to services and observe the
Sabbath while there are fields to be tilled, and his father is appalled
at Arieh's new, wicked ways. Jo comes to see Arieh again and tells
his brother that the people no longer support a man who cannot
keep his promises to them, and that he has received all of the help
that the organizations are willing to give him; he has lost his position as Prophet. As Jo sees the situation, only prestige concerns
Arieh. Jo has come to collect the debt that his brother owes
him—and he must collect it while Arieh still has some influence: as
a failure, he will be worth nothing to Jo. He wants Arieh's support
in helping him and Mr. Mordecai begin a conservative political party of their own. For Mordecai, it is a business enterprise to turn
Israel into a Capitalistic society with restrictive immigration laws.
Arieh is irrevocably opposed to the plan, and to Jo, who is always
the stumbling block between him and his visions. In addition to the
arms that Jo supplied in the past, he now offers Arieh the machinery
that he can obtain nowhere else to keep his settlement afloat. Jo will
even supply engineers and most of all, water. As Arieh is praying to
God for direction, Jo slaps him, throws him across a table, and
claims credit for Arieh's being in Israel. Arieh agrees to let the people of the settlement decide whether or not to accept Jo's deal, and
the scene ends with Arieh praying for a curse on Jo that will follow
him to his grave.

The final scene takes place in the same room that night. Mr.
Mayer bemoans to the rabbi how both of his sons are a disappoint-

ment for him: Jo because he hates his father; Arieh because he killed savagely on the battlefield, and Mayer fears him. When Arieh asks for his father's opinion, Mayer speaks in favor of Jo's plan, which will improve life in Israel; the people will live with dignity and not like animals. Arieh sees no hope and thinks that he has been abandoned by God as well as by his wife. Jo presents the alternatives to the members of the *kibbutz:* they can accept his help and become an up-to-date settlement or reject it and go on living in misery. In speeches of overwhelming emotional impact, Saul and Kulli speak against any plan that will keep their Jewish brothers and sisters our of the Promised Land. All pledge to support Arieh. In another emotional speech, Arieh recalls the history of ancient Israel and he is overcome with passion and with hate against his brother, who contradicts the mission of the Promised Land. Arieh strangles Jo, and Kulli, like Mr. Mayer, remains incredulous, stunned with grief. Arieh believes that God brought his hands to Jo's throat, but now Arieh must suffer punishment for the act. Saul takes command and orders Arieh to wait in his room until the police come for him. As the curtain falls, Mr. Mayer muffles the grief on his face in his prayer shawl.

Reduced to its simplest terms, "The Salt Land" is about two brothers, each with a dream for the State of Israel, each with an ulterior motive: Arieh, who wants to recreate the Garden of Eden in the middle of the Negev desert, but whose motivations are pride and stubbornness; and Jo, who wants to see the people of Israel living with dignity, but who is motivated by ambition and greed. It is the story of a father who suffers disillusionment over his sons: one because he has turned to crime in order to realize his dream, and the other because he comes to put material goals before Jewish law. And it is about a young wife watching her husband—and her marriage—falling apart.

The script that is no longer available is entitled "Balance of Terror," which was aired by BBC television on November 21, 1957, and then on "Studio One" in the United States on January 27, 1958. The BBC explains that their contractual agreement obligated them to erase the tapes and destroy the scripts. The following description of the play appeared in the *New York Times* on January 28, 1958:

International intrigue also was involved somewhat in "Balance of Terror" on "Studio One" over Channel 2 [CBS] last night.

This was a drama purporting to tell of British intelligence operations against Soviet agents in Berlin. The presentation on a network television program of such an inept production, presuming to deal with as important a subject as control of intercontinental ballistic missles, was inexcusable. (p. 55)

Shaffer agreed with the *Times*'s evaluation of the rewritten American version, and is quoted as having described the production as follows: "The good guys were clean-limbed, overgrown Boy Scouts. The bad guys were wicked, dreadful Communist agents. It was boiled down to the lowest common denominator of American television rubbish."[4]

The last play, "The Prodigal Father," was presented on BBC radio's "Saturday Matinee" on September 14, 1957. The play takes place in Glenister Hall, which has been in Lady Sylvia Glenister's family since 1670. It was built, much as was Shrivings, as a retreat from the cares of the town. There are eight identifiable scenes in the play, although they are not so designated in the script. The first is a conversation between father and son. Leander Johnson is considering buying Glenister Hall principally to give his son, Jed, some "class," which Leander feels is definitely lacking in his son's character. At once it becomes evident that the two are not comfortable around each other; there is no understanding between them, much less respect. The father's personal motive for buying the house is to try to make up to his son for the many years of neglect. Leander and his wife were separated when Jed was only four, and since then Jed was reared by just his mother in America, while Leander was off in Europe; this is the first time father and son have been together in sixteen years, and Jed does not let his father forget it.

The second scene introduces Lady Glenister, who is upset about having to sell the family manse, which she can no longer afford to maintain. Rather than giving us any information about Lady Glenister's past, the scene fills in more information about Leander's character. Jed's bitterness toward his father arises from having been deprived by him of a real home. While Jed accuses his father of pretentiousness, Leander rebuts Jed, accusing him of trying to be too manly, wanting everything that is the coolest, the latest, the snazziest. Jed fled five years ago at the time of his mother's death, and Leander spent those years trying to locate him. Leander is ready to unburden himself to Sylvia, to reveal the sordid details of

his childhood. It was his father who made the money, and he merely inherited it. His childhood was far from being happy: Leander's
mother died when he was eleven years old, and his father moved to
the American Midwest with him, a move which left the youngster's
aspirations totally unfulfilled. At eighteen, he ran away from his
father to realize his frustrated dreams. When he married, Leander's
wife wanted a rustic life, but his dreams were grander than that.
Nevertheless, Sylvia has more respect for Jed's honesty toward life
than for Leander's airs. All that Sylvia reveals about her life is that
she never had children and that she brought up Lucy, whose
parents were killed in an accident.

The third scene is between Jed and Lucy. Jed has gone through
life feeling that he was a mistake as far as Leander was concerned.
He admits that his self-image is very low; he considers himself a
moron because he does not have interests such as the study of
history. Jed's attention now turns to Lucy's problem: he suspects
that Sylvia never lets her out of the house. Lucy will not explain
herself and draws away when Jed tells her that she is pretty.

The fourth scene returns to Lady Glenister and Leander, and this
time it is she who talks of her past. After her husband died, she
spent a good deal of her time traveling, just like Leander. She was
lonely, and when the opportunity to rear Lucy presented itself, she
seized it. Sylvia's insight is more penetrating than Leander's and, at
the risk of not selling her house, she tells him that it is not a house
that Jed needs, but a sense of security.

The fifth scene adds no new information about the personal lives
of the characters, but in the final three scenes the denouement
proceeds rapidly. Leander is going to forget about buying Glenister
Hall in order to go back to America with his son and start over
again; for the moment at least, father and son have reconciled their
differences. Jed wants Lucy to see him again, but she does not
agree; Jed knows it is because of Lucy's sense of obligation to
Sylvia. Lucy does consent to write to Jed, and this is supposed to
leave their relationship on a hopeful note. Likewise, Leander wants
to see Sylvia again. In the final moments, Sylvia tells Lucy that she
thinks it is time that they have weekend company, her way of let-
ting Lucy know that the outside world is now welcome in her home.
Lucy, of course, is delighted.

"The Prodigal Father" is a bridge from an historical drama and
an espionage thriller to Shaffer's *bona fide*, serious dramatic
writing, which begins in the following year with *Five Finger Exer-*

cise. If "The Prodigal Father" seems to have too happy an ending and to be too pat, critical appraisal of the script must take into consideration its function of filling a spot on a Saturday afternoon radio program and not of being a believable piece of theater. The father-son relationship as described in "The Prodigal Father" is one of the axes on which all of Shaffer's drama revolves, beginning with *Five Finger Exercise* and continuing through his most recent works. To some extent, the figure of the father in this play is to become the figure of the mother in *Five Finger Exercise*: both of them are pretentious souls, impressed by wealth and stature. Young women often play marginal roles in Shaffer's plays, and Lucy is typical: she is young, attractive, and appealing to Jed. She is not an individual, but rather any woman to whom Jed could be attracted, and she refuses the attention of a young man abandoned emotionally by his father. Finally there is Lady Sylvia Glenister, mature, perceptive, and in many ways Leander's double. She is the outsider who unites the family, if only temporarily.

IV *A Pantomime*

The Merry Roosters' Panto is the only work written after *Five Finger Exercise* included in this chapter. It is a Christmas pantomime for children, produced at Wyndham's Theatre by the Theatre Workshop Company.[5] As with "Balance of Terror," for which the script is no longer extant, information on this play is available only from secondary sources. The play (which calls for the participation of the children in the audience) is Shaffer's interpretation of the Cinderella story, in which Prince Charming is a spaceman, the Fairy Godmother is the Duchess of Margate, Cinderella is a blonde suburbanite, and her stepsisters are played by men. Lionel Bart wrote the lyrics and Stanley Myers set them to music for the slapstick entertainment. Not all reviewers were in agreement about the pantomime. Philip Hope-Wallace in the *Guardian*[6] thought it was a spirited little show, while T. C. Worsley in the *Financial Times*[7] found it to be a dismal failure and did not even mention Shaffer's name in the review. Hubert Kretzmer, critic for the *Daily Express*,[8] saw an underlying moral in the work: why *should* Cinderella get to go to the ball? Has she *earned* the rights of leisure? Kretzmer's interpretation is in keeping with Shaffer's purpose in writing the pantomime. Also there is disagreement on the issue of whether or not the musical is for children. W. A.

Darlington, writing in the *Daily Telegraph*,[9] found it very much for children, but Milton Shulman in the *Evening Standard*[10] wrote that it was more for adult tastes than for children's, and a blurb in the theater section of the *Observer* alerts that "private and progressive jokes may deter some parents, but plenty of audience participation for non-political children."[11]

V *Summation*

Some of the works treated in this chapter may not seem of much importance in and of themselves. They are generally early attempts at writing—for radio, for television, for children's entertainment. Their shortcomings aside, the works do have value taken in the context of Shaffer's *opera:* from the detective novels, Shaffer said that he learned a great deal about plot development, and from the radio and television scripts, he was able to make the leap to the serious stage. Most importantly, these early works contain the themes, the types, and the motifs which are prominent in the major works on which Shaffer's reputation has been built.

CHAPTER 2

Five Finger Exercise

E NCOURAGED by the success of "The Prodigal Father" and "The Salt Land," Shaffer decided to devote himself to writing a play for the London stage. He wanted his material to be of more substance than that of the drawing-room dramas and comedies on which the London theatergoers had been nurtured, but he knew that in order to keep the attention of his audience his medium had to be one with which it could feel comfortable. What he had to do was construct a play that *seemed* traditional and that brought his respected predecessors to mind, and yet maintain the integrity of his subject matter. The result of his efforts was *Five Finger Exercise*, which opened at the Comedy Theatre in London on July 16, 1958, and established Mr. Shaffer as a playwright of the first order.

I *Plot*

Five Finger Exercise, a play in two acts and four scenes, takes place in the Harringtons' weekend cottage in Suffolk, England, in the present. Act One begins at breakfast on a Saturday morning in early September and continues on a Saturday night after dinner, two months later. Act Two occurs on the following Sunday morning at breakfast and concludes that evening, after dinner. Shaffer describes in intricate detail the scene which serves as the setting for the entire play. It is a multi-level set in which the living room occupies the lower floor, and the hall and study room compose the upper level. The living room is well furnished and "almost aggressively expresses Mrs. Harrington's personality. We are let know by it that she is a 'Person of Taste,' but also that she does not often let well alone."[1] As the curtain rises, Louise is serving breakfast to her nineteen-year-old son, Clive, and she wastes no time in ridiculing her husband to Clive. When Stanley (Mr. Harrington) enters the room, Clive, who was previously described as nervous, feels even more so. The family disagreement this morning is over the necessity of a private tutor for their daughter, Pamela. For Louise it is essential, but as Stanley sees it, the only reason Louise insists is that "the best people have tutors, and since we're going to be the best people whether we like it or not, we must have a tutor, too" (p. 3). It is immediately apparent that the issue of a tutor is only the latest detail in a continual battle betweeen husband and wife—Louise's pretentiousness versus Stanley's commonness—which Clive describes as a battle between "the *salon* and the saloon" (p. 32).

Clive tells his parents that he was out last night reviewing a production of *Electra* for a magazine, and the quarrels start again: Louise feigns shock over Stanley's ignorance of the play; Clive has to justify his literary interests to his father; Stanley criticizes Clive's impractical nature and his "arty-tarty" friends. Stanley knows that his offer will be refused, but, in an attempt to improve his relationship with Clive, he invites his son to go shooting with him. Clive prefers to stay behind and help Louise clear the breakfast table and, on her suggestion, do the breakfast dishes together.

Pamela enters with Walter (her tutor) and tries to talk him out of her French lesson. She is interested in learning about his past life and tries to get him to talk about Germany, his homeland, and his family, but to no avail; he claims that he has no family besides the Harringtons and that England will be his home. Clive lets him know that he is doing himself no favor by allowing the Harringtons to "adopt" him in this way. Louise goes for a music lesson with Walter, and Clive plays games with the material in Pamela's history lesson. In the last moment of the scene, Walter enters the room, and Clive is upset by his presence.

Two months pass between scenes, and Clive is now a student at Cambridge University. In the interim, he has started to drink whiskey rather steadily; he has lost his interest in helping Louise around the house; and he had had a talk with the manager of Stanley's furniture company, during which he criticized his father's "grotesque," "shoddy and vulgar" products. Stanley is no more impressed by his son's life-style than Clive is by his father's furniture. Stanley wants Clive to be practical about the future, to make the right friends, to choose a profession in which he can make money: "it's the one thing that counts in the end" (p. 24). Clive has no such concerns and is happy to be at Cambridge where, he says, people "speak his language." In Clive's conversation with Walter, the subject, as usual, is filial obligation: Walter does not approve of Clive's disparaging air toward his parents and feels that children owe their parents respect. In contrast, Clive feels only scorn for his own parents. Louise talks to Walter of her French ancestry and of how she married beneath herself. She, too, wants to know everything about Walter—about his family, about his past. He insists that there is nothing to tell and reveals only that he hates everything German. When Clive enters, drunk, he sees Louise holding Walter's head in her hands. He ridicules Louise's family tree to Walter and again warns him about his family. Clive needs a friend badly and asks Walter to take a trip with him during the forthcoming vacation. Walter refuses; Clive insults him and resumes drinking. Stanley tries to have a heart-to-heart talk with Clive, an attempt which serves to reveal once again how much father and son do not understand each other. He sees his son crying and forces him to tell the cause. Clive lies and says that he saw Louise and Walter together intimately.

Act Two takes place the following morning. In the first scene, Pamela gets the chance to speak and to show how perceptive a young woman she is. She tells Walter that her brother has never had a girl friend (and only once a female acquaintance), and that her parents are always having a row that is not really *about* anything. Then she confides that Clive has a recurrent dream about Stanley's coming into his room while he is asleep and peeling the blankets from him one by one. Stanley is distracted today, and Clive is more uneasy than usual, to the point of being sharp even with Louise. She has no trouble in recognizing that Clive is jealous of Walter's relationship with her.

Pamela trips on the stairs, and Walter rushes over to help her. He picks her up and carries her in a way that makes her feel like a baby rather than like the young lady that she would prefer him to consider her, and she tells her mother that he makes her feel ashamed. Walter is clever and penetrating but never heeds Clive's warnings about the personality of the Harringtons and allows himself to feel too comfortable with them, even to the extent of giving them advice and revealing the skeleton in his own closet to Clive: he does have a family back in Germany; his father is a Nazi who worked at Auschwitz and who brutally beat him as his mother watched uncritically. Clive still insists that Walter must leave the Harrington home for his own sake. Now Louise has her chance with Walter and speaks to him tenderly, wanting to hear more than anything else that he loves her; what she hears instead is that he thinks of her as a mother. She is distraught, and try as she might to hide it, her bitterness is evident.

The final scene of the play takes place after supper, for which Clive never appeared. Husband and wife battle over who is responsible for Clive's state: Louise blames Stanley for unfatherly treatment of his son, and Stanley counters by accusing Louise of ruining him, by making him into a mama's boy and turning his son away from him. Stanley offers Louise the chance to ask him for a divorce, but the whole subject is "too vulgar" for her to consider. On the pretext that Walter is having a bad effect on Pamela, Louise asks Stanley to dismiss him from his duties. Stanley goes to Walter, is sidetracked into talking about Clive and what a bitter disappointment he has been to Stanley, and never accomplishes his mission of firing Walter. Once again Clive and Walter talk, and this time Walter reaches the heart of the problem: Clive has to be forgiving toward his parents and not hold them responsible that he "has no girl friend." Walter's advice to Clive is the same as Clive's to Walter: to leave the house and never come back.

Stanley verbally assaults Walter; he blames him for turning Clive into a "sissy" and fires him, not because he believes that he is having a bad effect on Pamela, but ostensibly because he thinks that Walter is trying to make love to his wife. (He later reveals that he never believed Clive's lie.) Furthermore, Stanley is going to see to it that Walter will never get his British naturalization papers, and Walter's pleading to the contrary is in vain. There is a rapid denouement of accusations and counteraccusations: Clive accuses Louise of being jealous of her own daughter, and Louise rebuffs him, insinuating that it is Clive who is really attracted to Walter. As the family squabbles, Walter tries to commit suicide in his room, and Clive prays for the courage for all of them to go on living.

II *Characters*

Five Finger Exercise is a play of individual and family crises —husband and wife, mother and son, father and son—and the relationship of each of the Harringtons to Walter. As such, the body of any study on *Five Finger Exercise* must focus on the characterizations. Clive's recurring dream which Pamela relates to Walter is a metaphor for Shaffer's mode of writing the play: just as Mr. Harrington methodically strips the covers from his son, so the playwright strips the characters of their facades.

A. *Act One:*

1. *Louise and Stanley*

There is not one happy marriage in all of Shaffer's plays, and the trend goes back even further than *Five Finger Exercise* to "The Prodigal Father." He portrays husbands and wives whose basic values conflict to the point that harmony is impossible, and the prototype is the marriage between Louise and Stanley Harrington. Louise is described as "a smart woman in her forties, dressed stylishly, even ostentatiously for a country week-end. Her whole manner bespeaks a constant preoccupation with style, though without apparent insincerity or affection. She is very good-looking, with attractive features . . ." (p. 2). The manner in which Louise dresses is indicative of her pretention: her home is expensively furnished; her son is going to Cambridge; her daughter has a private tutor. Her special pride is her French ancestry and her family background. She tells Walter,

You see, when I married I was a very young girl . . . I had hardly met anybody outside of Bournemouth [her home town]. My parents didn't consider it proper for me to run about on my own. And when I met Stanley they did everything in their power to arrange a marriage. You see, they weren't exactly very dependable people. My mother was an aristocratic little lady from France who'd never learnt to do a thing for herself. . . . Naturally, father had reservations about the marriage. I mean, socially the thing was far from ideal. . . . His people had always been professional men. Marrying me into the furniture business—(*with a faint smile*) well, was rather like going into trade in the old days. (pp. 27 - 28)

She entered into a marriage in which she felt that she was compromising herself and has spent her life proving just what a sacrifice she made in marrying a vulgar and common man, for whom she has felt nothing but contempt.

Stanley is described as "a forceful man in middle age, well-built and self-possessed, though there is something deeply insecure about his assertiveness" (p. 3). Unlike his wife, he is a down-to-earth, hard-working person, with no pretentions and no education. He denies his family nothing and receives nothing in return. It is Louise who is in charge of the household—with little argument from Stanley about their relative positions—and she is absolute in her control: authoritarian, scheming, and ultimately vicious. Just as she furnished her house in such a way that Stanley always feels out of place, so her whole *raison d'être* seems aimed at the same goal: she speaks of the theater, which Stanley has never learned to appreciate; she punctuates her speech with French words, which Stanley cannot understand; and she loves the house to be filled with music, which gives Stanley a headache. If Louise has no understanding of Stanley, his understanding of her is perfect: she has to do whatever will make her one of the "Best People."

The basic theme of their continual row is always the same, and only the details change. In the first act the topic of argument is the need for a private tutor for Pamela. Stanley complains, "What's money after all? We had a town place so we simply had to have a country place, with a fancy modern decorator to do it up for us. And now we've got a country place we've simply got to have a tutor" (p. 4). Stanley does not understand why the things over which Louise becomes so excited are considered cultural at all: plays about "people having their eyes put out" (p. 5), or the music that Pamela is learning to play on the piano. Of course, Louise can never seem to remember the name of that Greek play that Sir Laurence Olivier was in, or tell the difference between pieces of music by Bach and by Mozart, and she depends on her son for her knowledge of drama, music, or anything that is intellectual and edifying.

2. *Louise and Clive*

The emotion that Louise withholds from her husband she lavishes on her son, a "quick, nervous, taut and likeable" young man. What Clive has to do to remain in the number-one place in his mother's affection is to correct her errors uncritically, side with her against his father, and play verbal games with her:

CLIVE   (*rising*) *Votre Majesté*. My Empress!
LOUISE (*permitting her hand to be kissed*) *Levez!*
CLIVE   (*Moving down L of the table*) The Empress Louise, ill-fated, tragic, dark-eyed queen from beyond the seas. What is your wish, madame? (*He makes a low bow to Louise*) I am yours to command. (. . .)
LOUISE (*rising*) I've told you already, my little Cossack. *Sois content.* (. . .) Be happy.
. . . .
        (*They embrace very fondly*) (p. 8)

Another game that Louise likes to play is that of givng nicknames, and the one that she uses for Clive is Jou-Jou, aptly enough her little plaything. Not only is it fun for her to have a human toy, but games help her forget that she is old enough to have a college-aged son. For playing games like this with her, Clive is rewarded with her loyalty: she defends and encourages his interests, kisses the top of his head as she passes, and lays his napkin across his lap. But Clive's compliance with the ground rules that Louise has established is only superficial, and he wishes that he did not have to sacrifice his father in order to secure the love of his mother, but so it is. Clive is to be pitied for his relationship with his mother: Louise holds tight, psychological reins on him, and he plays along with her both for the security of her love and the safety from her wrath. Louise deserves some sympathy, too: her marriage is passionless, and she must express emotion where she can.

3. *Clive and Stanley*

Just as there is not one happy marriage in all of Shaffer's plays, neither is there a good relationship between a father and his son. In "The Prodigal Father," the distance was a physical one—Leander and Jed were on different continents; in *Five Finger Exercise* the distance is emotional: Clive and Stanley do not share each other's values. Shaffer's description of Clive specifies that he looks like his mother. He also acts and thinks like her, as far as Stanley can see. If the contention between husband and wife is a continuous conflict between practicality and pretention, with father and son it is one of realism versus idealism. Stanley is a good father, but, despite his concern with his son's well-being, conflicts arise between them, both because there are real differences between Clive and Stanley, and because Clive fears betraying Louise.

From the first scene, it is clear that Clive would like to get along with his father, but he just does not know how. He wants to support his father on the issue of the need for a tutor, but he has to be certain that he in no way contradicts his mother's point of view:

STANLEY [to Clive] . . . We don't send our girl to anything so common as a school. You like the idea, I suppose?

CLIVE *(eager to agree)* As a matter of fact, I think it's ridiculous—I mean, well—unnecessary, really. (p. 3)

When Stanley informs Louise that Clive agrees with him and not her, she presses Clive, and he avoids the subject:

STANLEY   . . . Clive agrees with me.
LOUISE   *(pouring coffee for Stanley)* Oh? Do you, Clive?
CLIVE   *(quietly)* Isn't it a little early for this sort of conversation? (p. 4)

Stanley is interested in Clive's plans for the future. He would like for his son to forget the nonsense of college and certainly of the arts. He urges him instead to become interested in business and in making money. Stanley questions Clive about his whereabouts the night before, and with some reluctance Clive reveals that he was reviewing a play for a magazine that a friend of his edits, and that he plans to study literature at Cambridge. Stanley would like to know why he would study anything like that, and Clive's answer is incomprehensible to him: "Well, because—well, poetry's its own reward, actually—like virtue. All Art is, I should think" (p. 6).

Stanley finally gets around to the real issue at hand, that of making money: "You don't seem to realize the world you're living in, my boy. When you finish at this university which your mother insists you're to go to, you'll have to earn your living" (p. 6). After a round about Clive's impracticality, the subject is his choice of friends, on which Stanley has definite views: Clive should be making contacts in the business world with people who can be useful to him and help him get ahead: "I mayn't be much in the way of education, but I know this: if you can't stand on your own two feet you don't amount to anything. And not one of that pansy set of spongers you're going round with will ever help you do that" (p. 6). Stanley may object to the "pansy set of spongers" as not being able to help Clive professionally, but his real concern is that a son of his should associate with people like the "arty-tarty boys," "giggling and drinking and talking dirty, wearing Bohemian clothes, tight trousers," as they hang around Chelsea looking down on people who have interests more important than "*operah*—and *ballay* and *dramah*" (p. 6). Stanley goes on until Louise intervenes on her son's behalf.

4. *Pamela and Clive*
Pamela, the fourteen-year-old daughter, "as volatile as her brother, and wholly without his melancholy" (p. 9), is the least-developed character in the play. The only two people with whom she converses at length are her brother and her tutor. Stanley seems too preoccupied with the problems of his son to give her much

thought, and Louise does not go beyond fulfilling her motherly obligations toward the girl and using her as a pawn for her own ends. Pamela feels affection and genuine respect for Clive, although her relationship with her brother is more frivolous than serious: they play verbal games with each other (not unlike the games Clive plays with his mother, but much more innocent); they speak to each other in make-believe voices; and Clive quizzes Pamela on history by making a game of it:

CLIVE   . . . Which was the most uncertain dynasty in Europe?
PAMELA   . . . I haven't the faintest.
CLIVE   *(as if reading)* The Perhapsburgs. . . . Thomas the Ten-
           tative—a successor of Doubting Thomas, of course—and—
           . . . Vladimir—the Vague. (p. 17)

Pamela and Clive's is the only family relationship in which there is love and respect for as well as an enjoyment of each other, and in which there are no ulterior motives.

5. *Pamela and Walter*
    Walter is the common denominator and the catalyst, the outsider who is all things to all people: a tutor for Pamela, a friend for Clive, a confidant for Louise, and a sounding board for Stanley. But for her light-hearted games with Clive, Pamela hardly speaks to anyone in the play except for Walter. She talks about everything to avoid her studies—American English, her friends, her family—but mostly she is interested in talking about Walter. Where is he from? What is Germany like? What about his family? She is a budding adolescent with interests more personal than French verbs. She speaks to Clive of Walter in superlatives:

PAMELA   *(listening)* He's the best, isn't he?
CLIVE   Just about.
PAMELA   Oh, you can tell. I knew just as soon as he came in the door.
. . . .
CLIVE   How d'you get on together?
PAMELA   (. . .) Oh, we simply adore each other.
CLIVE   Is he going to teach you anything?
PAMELA   (. . .) Everything, my dear. (pp. 16 - 17)

6. *Louise and Walter*
    Misunderstanding characterizes the relationship between Louise

and Walter. Louise is thrilled to have in her home an intellectual-in-residence to give her daughter private tutoring, to play music on the piano, but most of all to fill her own emotional gap, left by the rift between herself and her husband. Walter is "a German youth, secret, warm, precise but not priggish" (p. 9); he is a mystery and a challenge to Louise. Treating him like another son in her house, Louise gives him a nickname, Hibou, the owl, because of his appearance when he wears his glasses. But it is not as a mother that she wants to be regarded by Walter. She unburdens herself to him and speaks of her family background and of her marital problems, explaining that only for the children's sake does she stay with Stanley. She wants to know about his past, but all that he is willing to tell her is that his parents died when he was too young to remember them and that he was brought up by an aunt and uncle of his.

Walter also lets Louise know that he hates everything German: "I am German. This is not so poetic—even the name—I hate. . . . You are too good to understand what I mean. I know how they seem to you, the Germans: so kind and quaint. Like you yourself said: millers' daughters and woodcutters. But they can be monsters" (p. 30). To Walter, England is Paradise, and he wants nothing more than to become a British subject and spend the rest of his life there. Slowly, Louise leads Walter into talking about his feelings for her. She begins by recalling the day they met: "at that terrible cocktail party in London, [you were] standing all by yourself in the corner pretending to study the pictures. Do you remember? Before even I spoke to you I knew you were something quite exceptional. (. . .) I remember thinking—'Such delicate hands—and that fair hair—it's the hair of a poet. And when he speaks, he'll have a soft voice that stammers a little from nervousness, and a lovely Viennese accent . . . [sic]' " (pp. 29 - 30). Walter bends and kisses Louise's hands, just as Clive does when he is game-playing with his mother. This is Louise's opportunity to establish the relationship that she wants with Walter, and she acts upon her desires: she takes his head in her hands and holds it close to her and speaks to him tenderly just as Clive enters the room.

7. *Clive and Walter*

Walter's presence in the Harrington home has its influence on the whole family, but more so on Clive than on the others: his effect on Stanley is minor; Louise is strong enough to recover from any disappointments she suffers because of him; Pamela is too young and emotionally immature to take him seriously. Such is not the situation with Clive: he has not yet defined himself in adult terms, independent of his mother's subtle pressures that he never grow up, and of his father's that he start accepting adult responsibility and thinking about the future. Walter's presence in the house is a source of relief at the same time that it is a threat and a torment for Clive. In their first conversation, Clive warns Walter about the family with which he is living: "This isn't a family. It's a tribe of wild cannibals. (. . .) Between us we eat everyone we can. . . . Actually, we're very choosy in our victims. We only eat other members of the family" (pp. 13 - 14). Clive, who has always had a family to take care of him, has been spoiled by it and can see only its shortcomings. Walter, on the other hand, considers himself fortunate to be living with a family and to feel the security of a home for the first time.

Jealousy, at first subdued and later pronounced, mars their friendship, as Walter, the intruder, threatens Clive's relationship with his mother. Rather than coming to Clive now when she has questions about music, Louise goes to Walter, who should know. (After all, he is German, which is almost Viennese.) When Louise decides to give Walter a nickname, just as she has given one to Clive, and she selects Hibou, Clive suggests instead "Pou" as being even better: it means "Louse."

8. *Clive, Act One, Scene Two*

Two months pass between the two scenes of Act One, and they are crucial months in Clive's life: he has started college, and being away from home has produced profound changes in him. The most dramatic change at home is in his relationship with his mother, who is now critical of him for taking so late a train that he missed dinner (she had prepared all of his favorites); for leaving his suitcases in the dining room rather than putting them in his room; for drinking more whiskey than she approves of; and for not trying to learn to play the piano. The first real blow to Louise comes when Clive is no longer interested in helping her with the dinner dishes; it is the first sign in Clive's behavior that he is asserting himself as an individual, unconcerned with his mother's disapproval. Her second disappointment is induced by Clive's reluctance to play their old games together:

LOUISE   Oh, Jou-Jou! *Mon petit Cossack. Embrasse-moi. (She pauses)*
            Non? *(She pauses)* It's your empress.
CLIVE   *(rising)* Your Majesty. *(He crosses to the sideboard and pours a*
            whiskey for himself) (p. 25).

And Louise exits into the kitchen. Later, on her suggestion that
Walter recite some poetry for them, Clive becomes furious and goes
out to a pub. When he returns, drunk, he finds Louise holding
Walter's head in her hands, and Clive is distressed.

What little there was of his relationship with his father has
deteriorated also. In the interim, Clive visited his father's factory
and was openly critical with the manager about the grotesque,
shoddy, and vulgar furniture that his father produces. Louise rushes
to Clive's defense: "Just because *you've* got no taste," she tells
Stanley, "it doesn't mean we all have to follow suit" (p. 21), which
she says as much to offend her husband as to support her son.
Stanley defends the practicality of his approach to producing furniture: he sells the people what they want and has been quite
successful; and he reminds Clive that his own business expertise has
kept the family well maintained. Clive is sorry for what he said
about his father's business and tries to apologize to him.
Characteristic of the good father that he is, Stanley is more concerned with Clive's life at Cambridge than with the incident at his
factory. Has Clive made friends? Joined any clubs? Participated in
any sports, perhaps? To Stanley's disappointment, Clive is active
only in the Dramatic Society. Stanley turns the conversation to what
Clive is making of his education, and Clive's poetic explanation is
not what Stanley had hoped to hear:

Look, education—being educated—you just can't talk about it in that way.
It's something quite different—like setting off on an expedition into the
jungle. Gradually, most of the things you know disappear. The old birds fly
out of the sky and new ones fly in you've never seen before—maybe with
only one wing each. Yes, it's as new as that. Everything surprises you. Trees
you expected to be just a few feet high grow right up over you, like the
nave of Wells Cathedral . . . [*sic*]. Anyway, if you had seen all this before,
you wouldn't have to go looking. I think education is simply the process of
being taken by surprise, don't you see? (p. 23)

No, Stanley does not see it. This is the time for Clive to be making the right friends, not just because he will be judged by the company he keeps, but also because the contacts that he makes now can

help him professionally later. The question of who are Clive's friends is touchy for him ("Do you want a list?" p. 23), and this scene with his father is an unpleasant reliving for Clive of his life before he started college. Clive goes through another round of trying to explain to his father who are the people that he, Clive, considers important, like a fellow student from Bombay: "He's completely still. . . . I mean that deep down inside him there's a sort of happy stillness that makes all our family rows and raised voices seem like a kind of—blasphemy almost. That's why he matters—because he loves living so much. Because he understands birds and makes shadow puppets out of cardboard, and loves Ella Fitzgerald and Vivaldi, and Lewis Carroll . . ." (p. 36). Stanley is both bewildered and impatient. He tries to tell Clive that he is happy that his son has some nice friends, and Clive accuses him of being patronizing. He is tired of being the one who has to try to understand his father; why does his father not try to understand him sometimes? Why must he be considered no more than an extension of his father rather than an individual in his own right, complete just as he is right now?:

I am myself. Myself. Myself. You think of me only as what I might become. What I might make of myself. But I am myself now—with every breath I take, every blink of the eyelash. The taste of a chestnut or a strawberry on my tongue is me. The smell of my skin is me, the trees and sofas that I see with my own eyes are me. You should want to become me and see them as I see them—as I should with you. But we can never exchange. Feelings don't unite us, don't you see? They keep us apart. (p. 38)

Clive is naive not to realize that it is precisely this kind of language that keeps him and Stanley apart because Stanley cannot begin to understand what his son means. Stanley sincerely tries to get closer to him; he asks if he would like to go over to visit a friend of his father and maybe stop off for a drink on the way. But Clive excuses himself on the pretext that he has some reading to do, and Stanley leaves discouraged. When he returns, Clive tells him dramatically, tearfully, and deceitfully that he caught Walter and Louise together; she was half undressed and Walter was kissing her on the mouth and on the breasts.

Jealousy gets the best of Clive when he finds Walter with his head in Louise's hands, and he cannot find it in him to be cordial any longer. He alludes to Walter's unkempt state: "Hair is being worn dishevelled this year. The Medusa style. What would have

happened if Medusa had looked in a mirror? Are monsters immune
against their own fatal charms?" (p. 31). And then he attacks his
mother's ancestors to Walter, to set the record straight on the half-
truths that Louise must have been telling him:

In actuality, I regret to say, they weren't as aristocratic as all that. My
great-grandpa despite any impression to the contrary, did not actually grant
humble petitions from his bedside—merely industrial patents from a run-
down little office near the Louvre. The salary was so small that the family
would have died of starvation if Helene, my grandmother, hadn't met an
English solicitor on a cycling tour of the Loire, married him, and exchanged
Brunoy for Bournemouth. Let us therefore not gasp too excitedly at the
loftiness of mother's family tree. Unbeknownst to father it has, as you will
see, roots of clay. (p. 31)

So much for his mother's family; now for his mother: she suffers
from what Clive calls a "plaster-gilt complex," and imagines herself
"ormolu" in a sitting room of plaster gilt; the only place she feels
really at home is in a *salon,* because there is no other place where
she can be so continuously dishonest. And why does she have
Walter in her household? Because he is a precious ornament, a dear
little Dresden owl, who sooner or later will be used and then cast
out when he can no longer help one member of the family score a
point against the others.

When Pamela comes home, Clive can only think: *"(to himself)*
She's the only one who's free, with her private star of Grace.
(louder) It's a marvelous dispensation: to escape one's inheritance"
(p. 33). For all of his lofty ideas, he envies his sister for the freedom
to be herself, just as he envies his friend from Bombay for his inner
peace.

Clive's attitude toward Walter changes, and he asks Walter to go
away on a vacation with him, maybe to the West Country at Christmas time. Walter refuses because he does not want to be away from
the family then, and he has his tutoring obligations for which he has
been paid until the end of January; besides, he has an obligation to
Mrs. Harrington. Clive pleads in quiet desperation: "If you come
away with me, it would be for my sake not yours. I need a friend so
badly" (p. 34). Walter pities Clive but does not change his decision,
and Clive lashes out against him:

Is that all you can say—"I'm sorry?" Such an awkward position I put you
in, don't I? The poor little immigrant, careful not to offend. So very sen-

sitive. *(with sudden fury)* When the hell are you going to stop trading on your helplessness—offering yourself all day to be petted and stroked? Yes! Just like I do . . . [*sic*]. O.K., you're a pet. You've got an irresistible accent. You make me sick!" (p. 34)

Walter excuses himself from the room as Clive tries to apologize.

B.   *Act Two*
    Act Two is built upon the conversations that each member of the Harrington family has with Walter. He has become more important in their lives, more a part of the family, and at the same time he remains enough of an outsider to be considered an objective observer by his confidants.

1.   *Pamela and Walter*
    The conversation that Pamela has with Walter begins appropriately enough as one between pupil and tutor and then proceeds to become more encompassing and more penetrating. In it, Pamela shows that she is an intelligent observer and a force to be reckoned with, not a silly child whose thoughts are dismissed by her mother (though not by her brother) as insignificant and unworthy of consideration. It is a Sunday morning, and Pamela, who is dressed in her jodhpurs for riding, demonstrates her interest in sports—an interest not shared by her brother. She reads the word *salacious* in the *Sunday Times*, and Walter tells her what it means. She thinks that he is brilliant and ought to be teaching English. Gradually, though not at all cautiously, she brings the conversation around to her family:

PAMELA   *(impulsively)* Are you happy here? Are you really, really happy?
WALTER   Of course.
PAMELA   Who do you like best?
WALTER   You.
PAMELA   No, seriously.
WALTER   I like you all. You and your mother . . . [*sic*]
PAMELA   And Clive?
WALTER   Of course, and Clive. (p. 42)

Walter feels sorry for him because he is so unhappy, but Pamela attributes his unhappiness to his having been spoiled when he was young. She thinks marriage would be the best thing for her brother, and that Walter must help him find a girl friend:

WALTER   Has he not had friendships with girls before?
PAMELA   *(in her affected voice)* Not even acquaintances, my dear. *(in her normal voice)* Except one . . . Clive said they used to go down on the beach and neck, but I bet he was just bragging. (p. 42)

Pamela suggests that Clive needs a girl who will pay attention to him because, as his sister sees it: "Clive spends his whole time not being listened to" (p. 43). Furthermore, she thinks (and Clive later reveals) that he is no more than a weapon that mother and father use in their ongoing battle, and: "With mother and daddy the row is never really *about*—well, what they're quarrelling about. I mean—behind what they say you can feel—well, that mother did this in the past, and daddy did that. I don't mean anything *particular*" (p. 43). Pamela tries to see her parents objectively without judging, and believes that each has a legitimate complaint against the other:

I know mother's frightful to him about culture, and uses music and things to keep him out—which is terrible. But isn't that just because *he* made *her* keep out of things when they were first married? You know he wouldn't even let her go to concerts and theatres although she was dying to, and once he threw a picture she'd bought into the dustbin. . . . But then, mightn't *that* just have been because being brought up by himself he was afraid of making a fool of himself. Oh, poor daddy. Poor mother, too. (p. 43)

Pamela gives details and a point of view on her family's struggles not heard from the other members of her family; and her concern is her family, not herself.

Later in the act, Pamela trips on her way down the stairs, and Walter rushes over to help her. Unfortunately, his manner of helping does not conform to her romantic fantasies about him, and she complains to her mother:

PAMELA   *(exasperated)* . . . And that idiot Walter has to come in and pick me up as if I was a chandelier or something. Holding me that way.
LOUISE   *(carefully)* What way, darling?

PAMELA   Well, trying to carry me, as if I was a baby. (p. 51)

Pamela regrets what she said about Walter and hopes that he did not hear any of it. It has, however, been well recorded in Louise's memory.

2.   *Louise and Walter*
Just as in Act One, Louise finds a private moment with Walter. All of the preliminaries finished, all pretenses stripped away, Louise quickly brings up the subject of love and introduces one of the tenderest moments in the play:

LOUISE   *(warmly)* I don't believe you can ration love, do you?
WALTER   *(admiringly)* With someone like you it is not possible.
LOUISE   Nor with you, my dear. You know, last night held the most beautiful moments I've known for many years. I felt—well, that you and I could have a really warm friendship. Even with the difference—I mean in—in our ages.
WALTER   Between friends there are no ages, I think.
LOUISE   *(tenderly)* I like to think that, too.
WALTER   Oh, it's true. Like in a family—you never think how old people are, because you keep growing together.
LOUISE   Yes.

       . . . .
What's the matter, Little Owl, are you embarrassed?
(WALTER *shakes his head*)
That's the last thing you must ever be with me.
(WALTER *smiles*)
What are you thinking? Tell me.
WALTER   Some things grow more when they are not talked about.
LOUISE   Try, anyway. I want you to.
WALTER   (. . .) It is only that you have made me wonder . . . [*sic*]
LOUISE   *(prompting eagerly)* Tell me.
WALTER   *(lowering his voice)* Mrs. Harrington, forgive me for asking this, but do you think it's possible for someone to find a new mother?
(LOUISE *sits very still and stares at Walter) (He kneels beside Louise and puts his hand on hers*)
Have I offended you?
LOUISE   *(smiling without joy)* Of course not. *(She slips her hand from under his)* I am—very touched. (p. 58)

What she really is is very crushed, and much to Louise's dismay she is herself partially to blame. While she tries to interest Walter in her as a woman and thus fill the emotional void left by her husband's indifference, she is also playing the same game with him that she plays with Clive, calling him "Hibou" and "my dear boy." She is equating Walter with her son and making him regard her as a mother. She fulfills his need for a family but lets herself in for a serious disappointment. Louise is well versed in the art of revenge; if she cannot have Walter, neither can her daughter or her son. Walter tries to express his concern over Clive's unhappiness, and Louise dismisses him brusquely: "As you said yourself, you *are* only a new-comer to the family" (p. 59). Pamela has given Louise the excuse that she needs in order to get Walter out of the house. Her daughter regards Walter as she would a character in a Romantic opera who "should wear a frock-coat and have consumption," and as someone who always makes her feel "ashamed" (p. 52): he is having an undesirable effect on a girl who is at an impressionable age.

3.   *Clive and Walter*

The seeds that Shaffer plants in the first act come to fruition in the second. Thus Clive's sexual preoccupation, which is only hinted at earlier, becomes a focal point in Act Two. He is forced to come to grips with his ambiguous feelings toward Walter: on the one hand, jealousy toward the intruder on his private territory—his mother—and on the other, an emerging closeness that he feels toward the strange man now living in their house. Walter mischievously asks if Clive thinks that he will make a good father someday, but Clive is feeling too cheerful for so deep a conversation. Soon his briskness and gaiety wane, and he talks about his future, which seems dim to him because he can identify only those things that he does not want to be in life and has no idea of what he does want to be. Clive is still waiting for his calling, aware that if he does not decide for himself how he wants to spend his life, other people will spend it for him. His self-doubts begin to surface: "I always seem to be talking about things that don't matter" (p. 55). He does not say this as an appeal for sympathy but out of conviction, hoping for Walter to supply an answer. There is a pause, and Walter changes the subject by apologizing for walking out on Clive last night. He thinks that it was kind of Clive to suggest that they take a vacation together and he encourages him to talk about the things that he has on his mind. Clive would rather forget those issues, and, making an about-face from the stand he took last night, he asks Walter to leave the house, to go back to Germany, to leave the Harringtons for his own good. If Walter will not go for his own sake, then he should do it for Clive's, who can't bear to watch. Clive never finishes his thought, but there are any number of things he cannot bear to watch: Louise's emasculation of Walter, or her affection for him, or Clive's own attraction to the man.

Clive's cheer has now changed to depression, and Walter thinks that he has identified sexual self-doubt as the reason for which Clive hates his parents and himself. Walter reveals to Clive the details of his first sexual encounter. He thought that it would change him, make him a man, make him so strong that nothing could hurt him again, but it did none of those things. He wants Clive to forgive his parents for "being average," for any mistakes that they made in bringing him up that have resulted in problems for him, and to forgive himself for his real problem which, as Walter sees it, is having fears and doubts. Walter insists that "sex by itself is nothing, believe me. Just like breathing—only important when it goes wrong. And Clive, this only happens if you're afraid of it. What are you thinking? (*He pauses*) Please talk to me" (p. 69). Clive mistakes Walter's concern for pity, as he violently seeks answers: "What's wrong with me? . . . What have they done to me?" (p. 69). Walter, in his turn, now advises Clive that he must leave his parents' house and never come back: "At the end of term in Cambridge, don't come back here. Go anywhere else you like. Join your American friend singing. Go into a factory" (p. 69). Walter reveals what he wants out of life: a wife, children, and many English friends. Clive's desires are less concrete: he wants to fall in love with just one person and to know what it is to bless and to be blessed. Clive consents to take Walter's advice and quips about how they spend their time ordering each other out of the house.

Similarly, Walter is ready to confide his secret to Clive, a secret which apparently nobody else in England knows. Walter is not an orphan; his parents are alive in Muhlbach, Germany. And it is not surprising that Walter has suppressed the facts about his past: his father was a Nazi and one of the most efficient officers at the Auschwitz concentration camp:

He was a great man in town. People were afraid of him, and so was I. When war broke out, he went off to fight and we [Walter and his mother] did not see him for almost six years. When he came back, he was still a Nazi. Now,

everyone else was saying, "We never liked them. We never supported
them." But not him. "I've always supported them," he said. "Hitler was
the best man our country has seen since Bismarck." . . . Every night he
used to make me recite the old slogans against Jews and Catholics and the
Liberals. When I forgot, he would hit me—so many mistakes, so many hits.
(p. 56)

His mother worshiped his father. As he was beating Walter, she
would look away; her husband was only doing his duty. Thus,
Walter's denial of having a family and his hatred of everything German becomes understandable.

4. *Stanley and Walter*

Everybody's feelings have been exposed except Stanley's, and he,
like his son, turns to Walter. Walter is as nervous around Stanley as
Clive is. Stanley is concerned that his son may be developing a
drinking problem, and that Clive uses alcohol to escape from his
father. He presses for Walter's opinion on what he has seen of the
family's relations, and Walter is frank in his reply: Clive does not
believe that his father loves him; he feels that his father is judging
him when they are together; that his father considers him useless.
Stanley sees the situation from a parent's point of view: children are
the selfish ones; they think only of their own problems; Clive hates
him and thinks that he is too busy making money to care for his
family. He imagines that when Clive is looking at him, he is thinking, "How common he is" (p. 66). Walter urgently defends Clive: a
boy should not have to apologize for enjoying Greek or opera.
Walter oversteps his bounds when he suggests that Clive needs
help, and the angered Stanley tries to blame Walter for his son's attitudes. Once calm, Stanley reflects out loud on his life, in a manner
reminiscent of another father, Mr. Mayer in "The Salt Land":

What's it matter? You start a family, work and plan. Suddenly you turn
around and there's nothing there. Probably never was. What's a family,
anyway? Just—just kids with your blood in 'em. There's no reason why they
should like you. You go on expecting it, of course, but it's silly,
really. . . . You can't expect anybody to know what they mean to
somebody else—it's not the way of things. . . . Perhaps he'll make the
rugger fifteen or the cricket team or something—anything—and then his
first girl friend and taking her home—or perhaps just keeping her to
himself till he's sure. *(frankly)* But nothing—nothing. And now he hates
me. (p. 67)

He has spoken his mind, and now the subject is closed.

Moments later, in a rage, he returns to dismiss Walter as Pamela's tutor, and Walter suddenly is blamed for all of the Harringtons' problems. Stanley resents Walter for speaking so freely about his adopted family; for being partonizing with his employer; for turning Clive into a "sissy"; for advising Clive to leave the house and never come back; and finally for having a bad effect on their daughter (which Stanley admits that he does not believe to be true). Stanley brings the scene to a climax by revealing the real reason that Stanley wishes to get him out of the house: Walter is trying to make love to Louise. Stanley tells it to him as brutally as he knows how: "You filthy German bastard. . . . Once a German, always a German. Take what you want and the hell with everyone else" (p. 71). One cruel blow follows another: Walter finds it incomprehensible that his friend Clive would betray him to Stanley by saying that he was making love to Louise. Worst of all Stanley will see to it that Walter is made to leave England for alleged indiscretions with Pamela:

I'm going to fix it so you never get your naturalization papers. I'm going to write to the immigration people. I'll write tonight, and tell them all about you. I'll say—let's see: "Much though I hate to complain about people behind their backs, I feel it my duty in this case to warn you about this young German's standard of morality. Whilst under my roof, he attempted to force his attentions on my young daughter, who is only fourteen." Try to get your papers after that. They'll send you back to the place where you belong. (p. 72)

Walter's every hope and illusion has now been destroyed: he has lost his "new mother," been betrayed by his only friend, been asked to leave the home in which he considered himself a member of the family, and been denied the chance of his becoming a British subject. He even now faces the most dreaded of all his possibilities, that of having to return to Germany. There is no reason left for him to go on living.

5. *Stanley and Louise*

In the last scene of the play, Stanley and Louise really discuss the family's problems. Since his conversation with Walter, Stanley is preoccupied with Clive and takes the offensive with Louise: "You know what the trouble is? Your son's turning into a drunkard," he says (p. 61). Louise counters by blaming Stanley for their son's drinking: "The way you've been behaving lately's enough to make anyone drink. . . . No-one would think he's your son. You treat him abominably" (p. 61). Tempers flare, but each one believes that he is speaking frankly. Louise believes that Stanley has made no attempt to understand him, and Stanley accuses Louise of turning their son into a sniveling little neurotic mother's boy, whose speech is starting to sound like that of a lunatic; it is all Louise's fault because every time Stanley tried to interest Clive in sports and thereby establish a decent relationship with his son, Louise interfered with excuses that Clive was too delicate and that his time was better spent reading. Stanley's closeness with Clive threatened Louise's selfish interests: if he had snipped Clive from her apron strings, she would have been left with nothing—no husband and no son.

Louise admits that she was afraid that Stanley would have tried to force him straight into his "third-rate" furniture business for the rest of his life: "Well, that's not good enough for *me*, Stanley" (p. 62). Whether it would have been good for Clive never occurs to her. After Stanley accuses Louise of destroying a son for him, Louise can stand no more. There is a moment in which, despite all of her flaws, Louise expresses seriously what has always been a thorn in Stanley's side, and she appears as a character who deserves some sympathy: "My life was never meant to be like this—limited this way. I know I'm unpredictable sometimes. I say things I don't mean. But don't you see I'm just so frustrated, I don't know what I'm doing half the time? . . . There are times I feel I'm being choked to death—suffocated under piles of English blankets. . . . I've never been able to take your world of shops and business seriously. Can't you understand?" (p. 63). Stanley is willing to offer Louise a divorce, but the idea is too vulgar for her to consider. He wants to improve their relationship (maybe a weekend away together would help), but Louise is not interested. Stanley worries about the effect that a divorce-would have on Pamela; Louise thinks only of herself and of Clive. She manages to change the topic to get Stanley to do her dirty work for her: she wants him to fire Walter on the pretext that he is having an adverse effect on Pamela. Stanley's unpleasant task of dismissing Walter is made easier once he has heard Walter express himself on how Clive is a troubled young man. And so Stanley does his wife's bidding.

6. *Louise and Clive*

The final confrontation is between mother and son, the two most explosive characters in the play. The scene brings to a culmination their disillusions compounded by jealousies and frustrations, and they show a complete lack of sympathy for each other. Clive has just returned home from a day's drinking, and Louise tells him that "your father and I have been worried to death" (p. 65). Louise's choice of words sparks Clive's jealousy, which knows no boundaries, and even extends to his own father: "Do I detect a new note in the air? Your father and I. How splendid! The birth of a new moral being. Your-father-and-I. When did you last see your-father-and-I? Or is it just a new alliance? All the same, I congratulate you. I always thought you two ought to get married" (p. 65).

Clive wants to know why Walter is so upset, and, although Louise does not want to discuss the matter, Stanley tells him that he has just dismissed him for paying too much attention to his wife, and Louise hears for the first time of the lie that Clive fabricated for his father's benefit. Clive still believes that "what I felt under the lie—about you and Walter—was that so untrue?" (p. 75). Now Louise's jealousy is activated as Clive expresses concern only for his father: "Can't you *see* what you've done? There isn't a Stanley Harrington any more. We've broken him in bits between us" (p. 75). What Clive wants to see is an end to the war that Louise and Stanley declared at the time of their marriage, the cultural war in which they use Clive as emotional ammunition. Louise tells Clive that Walter has been dismissed in order to protect Pamela, and he cries out: "*(in sudden despair)* He can't go away from here" (p. 75). Clive uses his strongest weapon against his mother when he accuses her of being jealous of her fourteen-year-old daughter: "What was it? Jealousy? Shame, when you saw them so innocent together? Or just the sheer vulgarity of competing with one's own daughter?" (p. 76). When Clive finishes his tirade, Louise bursts into tears, and Clive, desperate for tenderness, tries to resort to the reliable "French game," but he has gone too far, and even games do not help. Louise is provoked as never before; she circles her son, preparing to humiliate him by insinuating that he feels an attraction for Walter: "D'you think you're the only one can ask terrible questions? Supposing I ask a few. Supposing I ask them. You ought to be glad Walter's going, but you're not. Why not? Why aren't you glad? You want him to stay, don't you? You want him to stay very much. Why?" (p. 77). Clive panics, screams, falls across the table, and accuses Louise of killing him. While this scene is taking place in the living room, Walter is upstairs attempting suicide. Stanley saves him just in time, and Clive ends the play with a prayer: "The courage. For all of us. Oh, God—*give* it" (p. 78).

C. *Summation*

Except for Pamela, an innocent girl going through adolescent growing pains, no character is presented as all good or all bad. Louise is vicious, but she is suffering from cultural suffocation and lacks an outlet in her marriage for her emotional needs. She lavishes attention on Clive to protect herself from nothingness—to assure herself of a partner in her battle against the mundane. Stanley is the picture of the upright family man, but he is ready, based on a lie, to inform the immigration board of an alleged indiscretion and thereby ruin Walter's chances of establishing a life for himself in England. Clive receives a sympathetic treatment, but is guilty of deceit and of jealousy. Although he apparently feels nothing but love for his mother and contempt for his father, the situation is really more complex than that. Clive is a *poseur*, who, in his attempt to be liked, is whatever people want him to be: he plays games with his mother to keep her love, while at the same he harbors hate, jealousy, and resentment for what she has made of him. The contempt that he has been conditioned to feel for his father is really concern, and he senses an identification between himself and Stanley: both men are fighting to keep from being devoured by Louise. Walter's mask is the most blatantly misleading: he has been living a lie concerning his past, but only in order to protect himself from a world that would be harsh in its judgment of him and from a psyche which would otherwise be relentless.

III *Structure*

Characterizations aside, much of the beauty of *Five Finger Exercise* is derived from the simplicity, subtlety, and hence, elegance of its structure, which is faithful to the spirit of the classical unities. The play is divided into two acts, with each act divided into two scenes. The first scene of each act takes place in the morning and the second scenes take place after dinner. Two months pass between the scenes of Act One, but the effect of the play is that it

takes place in a single weekend. Each scene involves a series of conversations among the members of the Harrington family and the
tutor, with only a bit of new information given at one time, all of
which comes together in the climactic scenes of the second act.

Shaffer explains his intention in writing his first play as he did:
". . . I worked deliberately in the dead-ended convention of weekend-cottage naturalism in *Five Finger Exercise*, but without any
desire to be tricksy: the convention is utterly appropriate to the subject, and far from dead if handled with seriousness and desire.
. . ."[2] In another interview, he expressed his contempt for the
British drama that fails to go below the surface of family life: "I was
using the stock properties of the artificial, untrue and boring family
plays the English never seem to tire of in order that the audience
should feel solid ground under its feet and so follow me easily into
my play."[3]

The title of the play suggests a piano exercise for one hand, five
fingers, hence five characters,[4] and shows Shaffer's intention in its
structure. Each conversation, usually between two characters at a
time, is only moderately revealing as to the depth of intrigue within
the Harrington household, but like a good fugue, all of the elements
(here, characters) depend on each other, and thus the interrelation-
ships are shown to be mutually dependent: Louise's relationship
with Clive is more easily understood in light of her passionless
marriage; Clive's apparent scorn of his father is a consequence of
his relationship with his mother; Pamela is neglected because she
cannot serve as ammunition between Louise and Stanley as easily as
can her brother. Walter serves as a catalyst; all of the Harringtons
can speak freely to him, unburden themselves to him, and win his
sympathy. Thus, one and all use him.

IV *Critical Interpretation*

The play seems to be as straightforward as possible: it is a slice of
life on two significant weekends in the lives of the Harringtons. Yet
the reviewers and critics found all kinds of implications in the work.
For Gore Vidal,[5] the Harringtons are a family of stereotypes: four
strangers with nothing in common, forced by blood to share the
same house. Taking the Harringtons as a microcosm, he sees the
theme of the play as the downfall of the Western family. He takes a
dangerous critical position by projecting the Harringtons beyond
the limits of Shaffer's two acts, and he predicts that Louise will live

in a fantasy world that Pamela will marry, and that Clive will be a homosexual. John Russell Taylor[6] thinks that Louise is unjustified in seeing homosexual overtones in Clive's relationship with Walter, while the unidentified writer for McGraw Hill[7] maintains that it is Walter who encourages a homosexual relationship to develop between himself and Clive. Ignoring Clive's psychological problems brought on by his relationship with his mother, Kenneth Tynan[8] sees Clive as a rebellious youth fighting against a rich, philistine father. In a review in the *New Yorker*,[9] he expanded his interpretation to include that of five individuals in need of love, each one seeking it where it is least likely to be forthcoming. As such, it is a play of mutual incomprehension. John McClain[10] sees the theme as the inability of people to unburden themselves honestly to one another, an interpretation which probably comes closest to what Shaffer had in mind when he wrote the play. Loftus[11] quotes Shaffer on the play's meaning as that of a treatment of various levels of dishonesty. Robert Coleman[12] sees the problem delineated in the play as one of a lack of communication between the generations and jealousy between Louise and Pamela over Walter. George Wellwarth[13] probes an understanding of the playwright via his drama: *Five Finger Exercise* is Shaffer's attempt to exorcise his personal, drab, middle-class background by producing a work which denigrates his past. This interpretation is both speculative and nonliterary: the critic is not trying to understand a work of art, but rather to use it as a tool for analyzing its author. Shaffer views his play as "morally based": "It is about the fabric of life itself. Life itself is continuous." [14]

V   *Critical Acclaim*

Five Finger Exercise opened in London to enthusiastic critical acclaim and was an immediate success: Shaffer won the Dramatist Award of the *London Evening Standard* and the award for the Best Play by a New Playwright for the 1958 - 59 theater season from the drama critics of the London newspapers. Most reviewers were eager to praise the work and welcome the new playwright to the London stage. The *Daily Express*[15] praised Shaffer's flair for characterization and dialogue and called him an overnight great of the British theater. The *Times*[16] drew attention to the subtlety of the dialogue. The *Illustrated London News*[17] found in Shaffer's writing a feeling for phrase demonstrated by few other recent playwrights. And on and on. But there were also some critics who restrained themselves in their praise. *Punch*,[18] while it admitted that Shaffer had something to say and said it skillfully, believed that other reviewers were overly enthusiastic about the play. The *Spectator*[19] found the pace and bite of the dialogue to be praiseworthy, but criticized its lack of wit. In 1959, *Five Finger Exercise* moved to New York and received such an enthusiastic reception that, on December 4, 1959, the *London Times* included an article which echoed the New York reviewers.[20] The *New York Times*[21] was impressed by the subtle characterizations and the precise prose. The *Journal American*[22] found *Five Finger Exercise* to be nothing less than great theater. There was little dissension among the reviewers, and they presented to Shaffer the New York Drama Critics' Circle Award for the Best Foreign Play of the 1959 - 60 season.

The success of *Five Finger Exercise* is even more impressive and surprising when it is considered in the context of the historical moment of British and continental European drama. It was produced only two years after John Osborne's *Look Back in Anger*, which many authorities on British drama consider a turning point in the English theater.[23] It was produced in the same year as such "Angry" and revolutionary plays as John Arden's *Live Like Pigs*, Arnold Wesker's *Chicken Soup with Barley*, and Shelagh Delaney's *A Taste of Honey*. Shaffer's play was not only out of line with the British protest plays of the late 1950s, but was also in sharp contrast with the technically innovative drama being written by his British contemporary Harold Pinter, and such towering figures of European drama as Samuel Beckett and Eugène Ionesco.[24] The immediate appeal of *Five Finger Exercise* did not wane; it was produced as a film in 1962 and presented on the BBC "Play of the Month" in 1970. The play deserves its success and lives up to every line of praise bestowed on it by the critics. For its elegant structure, penetrating characterizations, and poetic and witty dialogue, *Five Finger Exercise* remains Peter Shaffer's finest play to date. There is not a play that Shaffer wrote after it that does not contain some element already found here.

CHAPTER 3

The One-Act Plays

Almost four years had passed since the respective openings of *Five Finger Exercise* in London and New York, before *The Private Ear* and *The Public Eye* debuted at the Globe Theatre in London, on May 10, 1962, and later opened at the Morosco Theatre in New York, on October 9, 1963. Shaffer wanted to experiment with new techniques and enjoyed great success with the variety of devices that he employed in his one-act plays. He also dispelled any ideas that he was a writer of only weekend cottage Naturalism. In addition to *The Private Ear* and *The Public Eye*, *Black Comedy*, paired in New York with *White Lies* and then in London with *The White Liars* (the final version of the play), proved that Shaffer was a master of a genre in which relatively few modern dramatists have managed to be successful with the critics as well as with the public. The plays are generally skeletal in their plots and are vehicles for Shaffer's character studies, themes, and techniques.

I   The Private Ear

The action of *The Private Ear* takes place in slightly over two hours in Bob's attic sitting room in the Belsize Park section of London. The room is shabbily furnished and dominated by the twin speakers of a stereo system. The argument of the plot is linear and simple: for the first time in his life, awkward and insecure Bob has invited a young lady for dinner. Lacking any confidence in his ability to prepare a proper dinner for her, much less sustain a conversation, he invited Ted, a more knowledgeable friend of his, to help him through the evening. Ted arrives a few minutes before Doreen is supposed to come and is disappointed to find that Bob is not dressed yet, that he has forgotten to buy an aperitif, and that he has no interest in any sexual activity with the young lady; he berates

Bob on each account. Ted shows Bob a photograph of the girl with whom he could have been spending the evening had he not agreed to help his friend. Bob upsets a vase, thus wetting the photo, which Ted puts on Bob's mirror to dry. Bob tells that he met Doreen at a concert; she dropped her program; he picked it up for her and asked her to have coffee with him after the concert. She accepted, and to his dismay, he could find nothing to say to her. Believing that she must share his love for classical music, he invited her for dinner.

When Doreen arrives, she is as nervous as Bob and not at all looking forward to the evening. Ted carefully combs his hair and comes in from the kitchen to serve wine. As is his custom, Bob does not drink. The conversation between Ted and Doreen is animated and slick, but when Ted returns to the kitchen to prepare dinner, Bob and Doreen are left alone groping to find something to say to each other. Bob begins talking about music, the only topic that he really knows. He speaks of his stereo set (which he has personified and named Behemoth) and of how pleased he is that Doreen was at the Bach concert. She confesses that Bach is not really her favorite composter; she prefers someone more modern, which Bob takes to mean Stravinsky and Shostakovich. No, she meant someone more tuneful; and Bob interprets this to mean a composer such as Britten.

Again Ted intervenes just in time to announce that the soup is ready, thereby saving Bob and Doreen from having to invent any more conversation. The dinner is painful for Bob. Ted begins by ridiculing opera and opera lovers, and Bob calls him "dead ignorant." Ted becomes more obvious in his attempt to win Doreen's affection, and Bob begins to drink wine. By the end of dinner, nothing remains of the wine or of Bob and Ted's former friendship. While Bob is in the kitchen preparing the coffee, Doreen confesses to Ted that she was at the concert by accident; a friend of hers gave her the ticket, and she did not want to see it go to waste. Ted slips her a pencil for her telephone number, and she excuses herself so that she may write it down. In her absence, Bob confronts a suddenly defensive Ted and orders him out of the house. When Doreen returns, she is unhappy that Ted left without so much as saying good night, and without her knowing where she can reach him.

As Doreen prepares to leave, Bob becomes urgent about losing her and makes attempts at telling her how pretty she is. He continues by telling her that he hates his job and confides that at times he spends his evenings "conducting" the records on the phonograph. Doreen is anxious to leave, but reluctantly agrees to listen to the love duet from *Madame Butterfly*, which Bob assures her will take only three minutes. In the six-minute pantomime that follows, Bob awkwardly tries to seduce Doreen and receives nothing for his efforts but a slap. Acknowledging his failure, Bob gives Doreen Ted's business address, which she had requested earlier, and lies by telling her that the photograph on the mirror is of his (Bob's) girl friend, to whom he is soon to be married. Left alone and desperate, he plays *Madame Butterfly* again and deliberately scratches the record beyond repair.

The Private Ear is a sensitive character study, and, as is the case with *Five Finger Exercise*, any examination of the play must focus primarily on the characters. Doreen is hardly developed and may be dismissed with little more than a casual comment. She is an antagonist, introduced in the play only so that Bob and Ted might have a chance to confront each other. Ted may not be dismissed quite so quickly as Doreen, but he is not so complex as Bob.

Like Clive in *Five Finger Exercise*, Bob is a discontented and confused young man, emotionally isolated and unable to communicate his feelings. His life consists of a job which he does not like during the day and of going to concerts or "conducting" his records alone in his room at night. On the evening that the play takes place, he is trying to change his patterns, to get acquainted with a young woman for the first time. In his imagination, he has idealized a work-a-day stenographer into the living image of Botticelli's Venus. All physical evidence to the contrary, Bob sees her as having "exactly the same neck—long and gentle," which is a sign of "spiritual beauty. Like Venus. That's what that picture really represents. The birth of beauty in the human soul."[1] Before Doreen arrives, Ted tries to make Bob see her more realistically, but to no avail, and the difference between his picture and her reality can cause Bob only disappointment. Ted also makes broad references to the sexual activity in which he expects him to engage Doreen, and this only angers Bob and makes him tell Ted things like: "Look, Ted, it's not that way at all" (p. 16) and, "Oh, Ted, I wish you'd stop talking like that" (p. 19). Ted accuses Bob of *wanting* to fail with women and he is right: Bob is not the first or the last young man in a Shaffer play whose sexual desires for women are, at best, minimal.

The feelings that Bob has bottled up inside of him are deeper and more spiritual than either Ted or Doreen can understand. Bob is unhappy and feels that his life is being wasted: "Some mornings I can hardly get out of that bed thinking how I'm going to spend the day. When I wake up I've got so much energy. I could write a whole book—paint great swirling pictures on the ceiling. But what am I *actually* going to do? Just fill in about five hundred invoices" (p. 53). He marvels at the miracle of creation and despairs at how people waste the precious gifts of life. In a poetic manner worthy of Clive Harrington, he expresses himself to Doreen:

Eyes. Complicated things like eyes, weren't made by God just to see columns of pounds, shillings, and pence written up in a ledger. Tongues! Good grief, the woman next to me in the office even sounds like a typewriter. A thin, chipped old typewriter. Do you know how many thousands of years it took to make anything so beautiful, so feeling, as your hand? People say I know something like the back of my hand, but they don't know their hands. They wouldn't recognize a photograph of them. Why? Because their hands are anonymous. They're just tools for filing invoices, turning lathes around. They cramp up from picking slag out of moving belts of coal. If that's not blasphemy, what is? (p. 53)

The object of Bob's worship is his music. He has not only personified his stereophonic equipment by giving it a proper name, Behemoth, but in the last scene, after he loses Doreen, he turns to his phonograph as if it were a lover or a god: "*He stands by it as it plays. He looks down at the record turning. He kneels to it, stretching out his arms to enfold it*" (p. 59). When he fails with Doreen, he turns against the thing he loves most, his music, and tries to destroy it.

Ted is the antithesis of Bob; he is "*cocky and extroverted, fitted out gaily by Shaftesbury Avenue to match his own confidence and self-approval*" (p. 13) and a self-proclaimed success with the ladies. He is also insulting and insincere. From the moment he enters Bob's room, he begins criticizing his friend: his forgetfulness and carelessness, his music and his clothes. Of Bob's ties, he says, "What is it? The Sheffield Young Men's Prayer Club?" and of another: "Look: that sort of striped tie, that's meant to suggest a club or an old school, well, it marks you, see? 'I'm really a twelve pound a week office worker,' it says. 'Every day I say, Come on five thirty, and every week I say, Come on Friday night. That's me and I'm

contented with my lot.' That's what that tie says to me" (p. 15). He
is just as unkind when he attacks Bob's taste in music, a very important and private part of his life:

> . . . Opera! How so-called intelligent people can listen to it I just can't im-
> agine. I mean, who ever heard of people singing what they've got to say?
> (*singing to the Toreador Song in* Carmen.) "Will you kindly pass the
> bread?" "Have a bowl of soup?" "Champignon"—"I must go and turn off
> the gas." Well for heaven's sake! If that's not a bloody silly way to go on,
> excuse language, I don't know what is. I wish someone would explain it to
> me, honest. I mean, I'm probably just dead ignorant. (p. 37)

His worst characteristic is his insincerity, his pretense at being a
friend of Bob. He claims at the beginning of the play that he refused a date with a particularly luscious woman just so that he could
come and help out his friend "Tchaik" on his first date. There may
never have been such an offer, and he might have thought that he
would take the opportunity to build himself up by knocking his
friend down, as well as to steal Doreen from him. He wastes no time
on either score; the moment Bob makes the mistake of offering
Doreen the Dubonnet that he has forgotten to buy, Ted appears
with a bottle of wine and asks: "Cocktails, madame?" (p. 29) and
continues with his charms to make himself attractive to her.

Ted makes his second appearance after Bob and Doreen suffer a
complete lack of communication regarding her taste in music. This
time he enters wearing a grocery bag, which is intended to make
him look like a chef. All through dinner he charms Doreen, as Bob
proceeds to get drunk. As soon as Bob is out of the room, Ted tries
to put Bob in a poor light in Doreen's eyes by revealing that she is
the first woman that Bob has ever had in his apartment. Ted's
cruelest cut of all is making Bob face himself during their final confrontation: "You *want* it all to be a bloody total disaster. Christ
knows why. Well, you've got your wish" (p. 50). Bob recognizes
how Ted has been using him and finally he reacts: "I'm just
someone to look down on, aren't I? Teach tricks to. Like a bloody
monkey. You're the organ grinder, and I'm the monkey! And that's
the way you want people. Well—go home, Ted. Find yourself
another monkey!" (p. 50). Ted shares some common traits with
Louise: affected speech and use of nicknames. As does Louise, Ted
spices up his speech with French, a word here, a phrase there, with
the intention of impressing Doreen, and to that end he is successful.

He also uses a nickname for Bob: "Tchaik," since Tchaikovsky was once Bob's favorite composer. The nickname is fitting, but also demeaning, both to Bob and to classical music, which Bob takes seriously. The kind of relationship that exists between Bob and Ted—somewhere between love and hate, admiration and ridicule—is a dominant theme in all of Shaffer's plays that follow (with the exception of *Black Comedy*, where the conflict between two men exists but only as a minor element in the plot).

There is no information about Bob's family, except that he has a mother who lives in Sheffield (no mention of a father), but there is some significant information about Ted's and Doreen's. Ted describes his father as "Mr. Alcohol, 1934" and as a man so completely dominated by his wife that he has not made a decision since he married. His mother is not much better: when she is not out at a bingo hall, she is at home with a bottle of gin. Doreen's father is much like Mr. Harrington, serious and practical, a man who spouts lines like: "Unpunctuality's the thief of time" (p. 24) and "Drink is the curse of the working classes" (p. 24). He is also a forerunner of the hard-working, Socialistic father in *Equus*.

Three dramatic techniques prevail in *The Private Ear:* music, tapes, and pantomime. The musical motif, well developed in *Five Finger Exercise*, plays a prominent role in this play also: the love duet of *Madame Butterfly* inspires amorous longings in Bob that he never knew existed and gives him the courage to attempt making love to Doreen. The music serves as a backdrop for a second technique, a pantomime, a six-minute sequence for Bob's fumbling attempt to seduce Doreen. (In this play's companion piece, silence is taken to its extreme.) Of at least equal importance is Bob's enthusiasm for Benjamin Britten and particularly for his opera *Peter Grimes*. What few details Bob tells Doreen of the opera mirror his whole life: a lonely man who has visions of an ideal woman. In the opera, Peter, a well-intentioned misfit, refuses the help of his friends, an action which gives added significance to Ted's final speech to Bob: "Don't lecture me, boy. It's not me who doesn't help. It's you, who doesn't want it" (p. 50). The use of tapes appears twice in Shaffer's dramas, in this, his first one-acter, and in his last, *The White Liars*. Its functions here are to speed up the time that passes on stage, to give a stylized appearance to the scene that is taking place, and to convey to the audience the drunken perspective with which Bob views the dinner-time conversation.

Criticism on the relative merits of *The Private Ear* and *The Public Eye* is mixed. For W.A.Darlington,[2] *The Public Eye* is clever and very funny but artificial comedy, and *The Private Ear* is a gem of writing. Emory Lewis[3] considers *The Public Eye* to be a vivacious work while *The Private Ear* is the more pensive piece. John Gassner[4] finds both to be expertly fashioned, but criticizes *The Public Eye* as being somewhat self-consciously cute and *The Private Ear* as being rather slight. For both J. C. Trewin[5] and Milton Shulman,[6] *The Private Ear* is the more successful of the two works. John Chapman[7] finds both plays silky smooth, literate, artful, witty, and irresistibly human. Some reviewers were so impressed with *The Public Eye* that *The Private Ear* seems the less important of the two plays. Harold Hobson and Hubert Kretzmer belong to this group of critics: Hobson[8] calls *The Public Eye* the "sure-fire hit," and Kretzmer[9] believes that Shaffer intended the more important piece to be *The Public Eye*.

The film version of *The Private Ear* was called *The Pad (And How to Use It)*.

II   The Public Eye

The Public Eye is Shaffer's contribution to European farce and deals with a problem as old as the genre itself: the young wife and the older husband. It is a straightforward piece, rich in the elements of traditional farce, from Plautus to Lorca. As in *The Private Ear,* there are only three characters, and the play is constructed on their mutual misunderstandings and the games that they play with each other. The comedy takes place in the outer office of Charles Sidley's Bloomsbury accounting firm. The office, well furnished and lined with books, reflects the presence of a prosperous professional. Julian Cristoforou, an eccentrically dressed man in his mid-thirties, is staring at his large turnip watch and mixing packets of raisins and nuts, which he produces from the large pockets of his raincoat. Charles Sidley, a meticulous man of forty, appears and is surprised to find someone in his office on Saturday. Sidley does not know Cristoforou, nor does he know why he has come to see him. Julian's remarks serve to enhance rather than diminish the confusion, in the ensuing conversation of noncommunication:

CHARLES   . . . Now, if you don't mind—perhaps I can make an appontment for next week.

JULIAN   (*ignoring him, staring at the shelves*) Websters! Chambers!
                Whittakers Almanac! Even the names have a certain leathery
                beauty. And how imposing they look on shelves. Seried ranks
                of learning!
CHARLES   (*brutally*) Are you a salesman?
JULIAN   Forgive me. I was lapsing. Yes, I was once. But then I was
                everything once. I had twenty-three positions before I was
                thirty.
CHARLES   Did you really?
JULIAN   I know what you're thinking. A striking record of failure. But
                you're wrong. I never fail in jobs, they fail me.
CHARLES   Well, I really must be getting home now. I'm sorry to have
                kept you waiting, even inadvertently. May I make an appoint-
                ment for you early next week?
JULIAN   Certainly. If that's what you want.
CHARLES   Well, as I say, I don't receive clients at the weekend. Now let
                me look at my secretary's book . . . [*sic*] What about next
                Tuesday?
JULIAN   (*considering*) I don't really like Tuesdays. They're an indeter-
                minate sort of day.
CHARLES   Would you please tell me when you would like to see me?
JULIAN   It's rather more when *you* would like, isn't it?
CHARLES   I suppose I could squeeze you in late on Monday if it's
                urgent.
JULIAN   I had imagined it was. In fact, I must admit to feeling disap-
                pointed.
CHARLES   I'm sorry—
JULIAN   No, if the truth be known, extremely surprised.
CHARLES   Surprised?
JULIAN   At your being so off-hand. I had imagined you differently.
CHARLES   Are you in some knd of trouble?
JULIAN   Your trouble is mine, sir. It's one of my mottoes. Not inap-
                propriate, I think. Still, of course, I mustn't be unreasonable.
                It's your decision. After all, you're paying.
CHARLES   I'm what?
JULIAN   Paying. (*He pretends to go out.*)
CHARLES   Mr. Cristoforou, come here. I had assumed you were here to
                see me professionally.
JULIAN   Certainly. (pp. 65 - 67)

And so the conversation goes in vaudevillian manner until Julian
lets Charles know that he is the private detective (public eye) from
the firm that Charles has employed to follow his wife and determine
whether she is being sexually unfaithful to him. In the month since

the detectives last reported to Charles, they have still found no reason to believe that Belinda, Charles's wife, is having an affair with another man. Julian has determined, however, that Belinda is seeing another man on a daily basis, a man whom Julian describes as handsome and debonair; a diplomat, perhaps. Julian does not know his name or where he lives. Charles becomes violent and threatens Julian with physical harm if he does not have more information on the man by nighttime. At this point, Charles hears Belinda approaching and orders Julian down the fire escape.

Belinda is a pretty young woman of twenty-two, who is wearing unconventional clothes—a characteristic which links her with Julian—and carrying an armload of flowers for her husband's office. Just as there was no understanding on either part when Charles and Julian were speaking to each other, so it is when Charles tries to get Belinda to understand what he considers to be the role of a wife: his definition is tight and conventional; his wife is neither. Charles claims that he loves Belinda very much, but she finds it hard to believe and denies that there is any life left in their marriage. Charles is hurt and announces that she is seeing another man. She tries to deny it, but Charles insists that she be as honest as she presumes to be and forces her to reveal the details of the relationship. Yes, she is *seeing* another man, no more and no less. He follows her all over London—to parks, cinemas, coffee bars—and in three weeks they have not exchanged a single word. The man, as Belinda describes him, is not handsome and debonair, but: "a goofy-looking man with spectacles, eating macaroons out of a polythene bag" (p. 96); Charles knows that she can only be describing Cristoforou. Belinda opens the door to water the flowers and discovers Julian, who has been eavesdropping on the entire conversation.

Belinda suffers two hurts in rapid succession: first, that her husband has employed a private detective to spy on her; and second, that Julian is being paid to follow her around London. She wants nothing more to do with either of them. Julian asserts himself: he orders Sidley out of his own office and orders Belinda not to speak to her husband for thirty days. As he sees it, without speaking, he and Belinda have managed to form a close relationship, and he believes that it can be the same way with Belinda and Charles. He tolerates no questioning, commenting, or interfering with his plan: Charles is to follow his wife around London for a full month looking at anything she chooses to point out: "Sit, stand, skip, slide, or shuffle entirely at her will" (p. 115). If Charles refuses, Julian will tell Belinda that her husband has been paying calls to a Notting Hill Gate prostitute (an idle threat, since Julian found out this bit of information from Belinda). Charles reluctantly agrees. And while Charles is performing Julian's job, Julian will perform Charles's: for the next thirty days he will play at being an accountant.

With the exception of Louise Harrington, Belinda is Shaffer's most fully developed female character and not a mere antagonist with whom the male characters may interact. Belinda spent the first eighteen years of her life in Northampton with parents whose ambitions for her were a job at the library and marriage to a local boy. Belinda rebelled by running off to London and moving in with two bohemian artists. When Charles met her, she was a waitress at a club in Soho. She was swept off her feet by Charles's encyclopedic knowledge, and they were married. She traded her circle of friends (which included an artist who spat paint directly from his mouth to express his contempt for society) for Charles's in the financial world, and the change has been impossible for her to accept. She refuses to submerge her individuality by renouncing her routine of seeing horror films and eating ice-cream concoctions, for cutting cigar ends and pouring port for old men. Within her value system, her time is better spent in concern over the plight of the Yaghan Indians of Southern Chile than in the routine details of keeping house. Like Louise Harrington, she was being suffocated in her husband's world of business affairs and had to break out. Her needs are diverse and cannot be satisfied by one man:

You've got to be faithful to all sorts of people. You can't give everything to just one. Just one can't use everything. And you certainly can't *get* everything from just one. Just because you get sex from a man, it doesn't mean you're going to get jokes as well, or a someone who digs jazz. Oh I know a husband claims the right to be all these things to a woman, but he never is. The strain would be appalling (pp. 91 - 92).

Charles is the most unlikely candidate as a husband for Belinda. He is a staid accountant, a man of the most traditional and conservative nature. He met Belinda when a friend of his invited him to the club where she was working. He married her with the idea of playing Pygmalion and of making her over in his own image, something that she pretended to want, and that he proceeded to do. Now, he claims the credit for everything she knows, from selecting hats to viewing statues. Charles says he was "infatuated" with her when they were married, and his reasons for wedding her were completely selfish:

CHARLES   . . . She was young and that was enough. Youth needs only to show itself. It's like the sun in that respect. In company with many men of my age, I found I was slipping away into middle life, journeying, as it were, into a colder latitude. I didn't like it. I didn't like it at all.

JULIAN   So you went after the sun. Tried to bottle a ray or two.

CHARLES   Foolish, imbecile attempt. Within a year I had to recognize that I had married a child. Someone with no sense of her place at all. (p. 81)

As Charles defines Belinda's place, it is at home, catering to his friends from investment companies in the City; behaving as the wife of a professional man and not as that of a "jazz trumpeter in New Orleans" (p. 82).

Charles began to suspect that his wife was seeing another man when, for the last three months, she completely avoided him: "Well, she is averting her face, her look, her mind. Everything. Whole meals go by in silence. . . . Now she's up and out of the house sometimes before eight. As if she can't bear to lie in my bed another minute . . . [sic]" (p. 83). There is a double standard in Charles's sexual attitudes: he complains that when Belinda was single she went to bed with three different men in the same week, but he, as a married man, has no trouble accepting his regular visits to a prostitute.

The presence of Julian Cristoforou turns domestic melodrama into true farce: *"his whole air breathes a gentle eccentricity"* (p. 63), his conversation borders on the absurd and no less so his manners and dress. He speaks in paradoxes, describing his name, Cristoforou, as a "little downbeat" and his appearance as "nondescript." He is well intentioned and yet confesses that his motives are somewhat selfish: after spending three years as a detective who broke up marriages, he would like to cement just one. But it is more than that: like Bob, he is a social misfit, and just as Bob hides from himself and from the rest of the world by conducting records in his room at night, so Cristoforou adopts a way of living that is compatible with his personality:

Most of my life has been spent making three where two are company. I was hardly out of puberty before I started becoming attracted to other men's

wives. Women who were unattainable obsessed me. . . . I was always in
the middle, getting nothing and being generally in the way. Finally I made
myself so unhappy that I had to sit down and think. One day I asked myself
this fateful question: "Would you like to know a beautiful, tender, unat-
tached girl to whom you were everything in the world?" And the answer
came back: "No!" . . . [*sic*] Revelation! At that moment I realized
something shattering about myself. I wasn't made to bear the responsibility
of a private life! Obviously Nature never intended me to have one! I had
been created to spend all my time in public! . . . Alone, I didn't exist; I
came alive only against a background of other people's affairs. . . . I immediately resigned from Private Life, and became a Public Eye. (p. 104)

The problem with the Sidleys' marriage is that it has lost the
spark that made it successful at the start—Charles is no longer attracted by Belinda's youth, and Belinda no longer worships
Charles's learning. Cristoforou is the personification of that which
can cure the ills of their marriage: a little imagination. As eccentric
as he may be, he is the one person who can reunite Charles and
Belinda; he has the creativity which appeals to her and the assertiveness which appeals to him. He has been successful at establishing a relationship with Belinda and now encourages Charles
to speak to him freely of his marital problems and personal shortcomings. In his attempt to save their marriage, the games he plays
with the Sidleys range from describing himself as handsome and
debonair (to make Charles jealous) to making idle threats of telling
Belinda about her husband's visits to a prostitute (to make him
vulnerable).

The situation on which the play is constructed fits within the
tradition of European farce; it is a *mélange* of the time-honored
tales of the old man in pursuit of the young girl, and that of the imaginative and spirited young wife married to a dull, lifeless, older
man. As such, Belinda and Charles Sidley are the two characters in
Shaffer's dramatic creation most profoundly steeped in literary
tradition. The greatest writers of comedy all tried their hands at the
problem. Plautus established the prototype of the *senex amator* in
Mercator (The Merchant); Molière adapted the situation for his
seventeenth-century *L'École des femmes* (The School for Wives).
In the eighteenth century, Regnard altered Molière's plot enough to
produce another masterwork of comedy, *Le Légataire universel*
(The Residuary Legatee). In *El sí de las niñas* (The Girls' Consent),
Leandro Fernández de Moratín, the most successful Spanish
playwright of manners of the eighteenth and early nineteenth cen-

turies, has a fifty-nine-year-old man in pursuit of a sixteen-year-old girl, to whom he would be more of a father than husband if the marriage were to take place. More recently, in the twentieth-century theater, Federico García Lorca uses the same plot in four of his fifteen plays, two of which were written for puppets—*Los títeres de cachiporra* (The Malicious Puppets) and *Retablillo de don Cristóbal* (The Little Puppet Stage for don Christopher)—and two of which were written for human actors—*La zapatera prodigiosa* (The Shoemaker's Prodigious Wife) and *Amor de don Perlimplín con Belisa en su jardín* (The Love of don Perlimplín with Belisa in the Garden). Throughout the centuries the moral of the play has been the same that Charles confesses to Cristoforou: "The moral, of course, is that men of forty shouldn't marry girls of eighteen. It should be a law of the church like consanguinity: only marry in your generation" (p. 81).

There is another message in the play, too: imagination and fantasy are essentials in life (especially in marriage) and they keep the everyday realities of life from becoming overbearing. Lorca has that same message for his readers in his poetic farce *La zapatera prodigiosa*, but the play that is the closest to Shaffer's is Jacinto Grau's *Las gafas de don Telesforo* (Telesforo's Spectacles). The name of the title character recalls that of the detective in *The Public Eye*, and Grau's comedy is subtitled "Farsa en tres ratos de la vida de un hombre singular" (A Farce in Three Episodes in the Life of an Unusual Man). The two men are similar in name, appearance, and function. Telesforo's prescription for solving problems is much the same as Cristoforou's, too: suspend reality for a while, let go, and allow the imagination to take over.

The Private Ear and *The Public Eye* share themes of misunderstanding, absence of love, loneliness, and fantasy. Bob invited Doreen to his flat for dinner because he mistook her presence at a concert and misidentified her as a music-lover. Similarly, Charles thought that marrying an eighteen-year-old girl would give him back the *joie de vivre* that the years had taken away from him. Neither woman understands what the men are trying to say to them. In both plays, the women are the innocent victims: Doreen subjects herself to a near-seduction, and Belinda, to a joyless marriage. There is an identification between Bob and the Sidleys, all of whom lead lonely and loveless lives, and even more strongly between Bob and Cristoforou, whose lives are little more than their fantasies: alone at night Bob privately imagines himself a conductor; and publicly during the day, Cristoforou plays at his various professions, from private eye to public accountant. Both Bob and Julian escape from the real world and hide from relationships with women: Bob retreats to his music, and Julian, to his professional games. Bob and Belinda are related, since each has turned himself over to another person (Ted and Charles, respectively) to be made over in the other's image.

Shaffer wrote his own screenplay for the 1972 film version of *The Public Eye*, also called *Follow Me!*

III   Black Comedy

Shaffer wrote *Black Comedy* under circumstances which normally do not appeal to him: a deadline, imposed by the National Theatre, directed by the then Sir Laurence Olivier. The comedy had its debut on July 27, 1965, on a program with Strindberg's *Miss Julie*. For the New York opening at the Ethel Barrymore Theatre, on February 12, 1967, Shaffer wrote *The White Liars* (originally called "A Warning Game") as a curtain-raiser. After a successful run in New York, with reviews that were as enthusiastic as those of its London premiere, there was a second London production which opened at the Lyric Theatre on February 21, 1968, accompanied by *The White Liars*, a rewritten version of *White Lies*.

The play is based on a conceit of traditional Chinese drama that when the lights are on onstage, the actors behave as if they were in complete darkness, and when the lights are off, they act as if nothing were amiss. Using a reversal of darkness and light, Shaffer created one of the best farces in the modern English theater. As in the previous one-act plays, Shaffer is faithful to the classical unities of time, place, and action.

The storyline is simple, but the confusion resulting from mistaken identities and misunderstood motives keeps the farce moving at a lively pace. The scene is the South Kensington, London, flat of Brindsley Miller, a sculptor in his mid-twenties, intelligent and handsome, but like Clive and Bob, nervous and unsure of himself. On the Sunday evening in question, Georg Bamberger, a millionaire art collector, is coming to inspect, and perhaps purchase, some of Brindsley's work. On the same evening, his fiancée, Carol, a silly and spoiled debutante, is bringing her father, the Colonel, to meet Brin and give his consent to their marriage. In order to impress Colonel Melkett, Brin has borrowed some of his neighbor's most treasured antiques. The neighbor, Harold Gorringe, is the owner of an antique shop and treats his possessions as if they were his children. Brin helped himself to Harold's treasures for the evening, while his neighbor was away for the weekend. At the height of Brin's anxiety over meeting Carol's father, nervousness over Bamberger's appraisal of his art, and fear of Harold's early return, a fuse blows. Until this point, Brin and Carol had been acting on a completely dark stage as if they could see perfectly: Brin compliments Carol on her yellow dress, which brings out the color of her hair; Carol tells Brin to straighten his tie because he looks sloppy. Now that the fuse has blown, the lights come up onstage, and the characters pretend to be in darkness.

While they are groping around for matches, Brin has a telephone call from Clea, his ex-mistress, who wants to come to see him. Brin has just lied to Carol that he has not seen Clea in two years, that their affair lasted for three months, and that she was "about as cozy as a steel razor blade."[10] He follows those lies up with another: Clea is "just a chum," he tells Carol. As Brin is about to go out to a pub for matches, in comes Brin's upstairs neighbor, Miss Furnival, the spinster daughter of a Baptist minister. As befitting her station, she is prissy, refined, and unaccustomed to alcoholic beverages. While Brin is calling the electric company for help and going to Harold's apartment in search of a candle, Carol informs Miss Furnival of the background of the evening. She also asks her to be a good sport and not divulge that Brin has borrowed Harold's china and furniture, which Miss Furnival recognizes immediately as belonging to her friend; this is Brin's only hope of convincing the Colonel that Brin can support his daughter.

During Brin's absence, the Colonel has also arrived and has begun criticizing Brin's lack of organization. Brin returns, not knowing that the Colonel has arrived, and refers to Carol's "monster father." From then on, it goes from bad to worse between Brin and Carol's father; in his nervousness, everything the young man says is wrong. Brin was unable to find candles in Harold's apartment and is now on his way to the pub, when he encounters Harold, who has returned unexpectedly. To keep him from discovering that the furniture is missing from his apartment, Brin leads him into his own flat. Thinking that they are alone and that he is finally going to get the attention from Brin that he has long wanted, Harold takes Brin's arm and mentions how cozy it is in the dark. To Harold's dismay, they are not alone, but he consents to stay for a drink. Brin uses Harold's raincoat to cover the Wedgwood bowl which he has taken from Harold's apartment.[11] Harold has matches, and each time he lights one, Brin blows it out so that Harold will not see the furniture. (When a match is lighted on stage, the lights dim a little in keeping with the complete reversal of light and darkness).

Without the benefit of light, Brin attempts to return Harold's furniture to his apartment without being discovered. In a desperate attempt to keep her father's attention away from her fiancé, who is being taken for a madman, Carol decides that it is time to serve drinks. Naturally, in the darkness they are all confused, and Miss Furnival receives a glass of scotch. She takes a long drink before returning it, and after having her first taste of alcohol, makes several trips to the bar for large doses of gin. The Colonel discovers that Brin is still in the apartment, and Brin feels compelled to say that he has been to the pub and back and that it was closed. The Colonel is enraged at Brin's lying and threatens not to let him marry his daughter. This is the first time that Harold has heard that there is marriage in Brin's immediate future, and he is incensed at not having been told before and about having to hear it in a room full of strangers. There is no making up to the moody Harold for keeping a secret from him.

In the midst of an already frantic situation, Clea arrives and in the darkness goes unnoticed. To Brin's dismay, the subject turns to his former girl friends, and he tries, none too successfully, to keep Harold from volunteering any information about Clea. But Harold is still hurt at having been slighted by his friend and speaks spitefully of how ugly Clea was: "teeth like a picket fence—yellow and spiky" and skin that was "like new pink wallpaper, with an old grey crumbly paper underneath" (p. 89). Miss Furnival joins in and comments not only on Clea's "lumpy" appearance but also on how "tiresomely Bohemian" she was. When Clea can stand no more, she takes careful aim and slaps Brin's face. Brin assumes that Harold slapped him, and further confusion ensues. Groping about in the dark, Brin catches Clea by the bottom, recognizes her immediately, and begins talking of how beautiful, witty, and loyal she was. He also takes the opportunity to start kissing her and to ask her to go up to the bedroom and wait for him to come up and explain. Harold, standing nearby, thinks that Brin is inviting *him* to the bedroom, but asks whether this is "quite the moment." In the bedroom, Brin lies to Clea about his relationship with Carol and about the purpose of her father's visit. He begs her to leave quietly and kisses her passionately.

As Carol is beginning to suspect that there is something going on in Brin's bedroom, Schuppanzigh, the electrician, enters, and since he has a German accent and a knowledge of art, he is mistaken for Bamberger and is treated accordingly. Bamberger is supposed to be "stone deaf," and so Brin, Carol, and Miss Furnival shout in Schuppanzigh's ear, and he cannot imagine what is happening. All gather to listen to him as if he were giving the last word on sculpture until he reveals his identity. He is assaulted with insults and goes through the trapdoor to replaces the fuse in the cellar. Carol mentions her forthcoming marriage to Brin, Clea's mouth falls open, and she is determined to have her revenge. First she takes a bottle of vodka from the bar and goes to the bedroom level from which she soaks Carol, Brin, Harold, and the Colonel. Improvising wildly, Brin tries to make his guests believe that the cleaning woman is upstairs and gets Clea to play along for the moment. Cautioning her to watch her language, the Colonel tells Clea that she is in the presence of Brin's fiancée, and in an inspired moment she asks: "You must be Miss Clea's father" (p. 109). Brindsley falls face down on the floor. She continues that it is a good thing that Brin finally asked her to marry him since her "little bun in the oven" was getting "a bit prominent" (p. 110). Clea reveals her identity, and by using Carol's affectations of speech proceeds to insult Miss-Laughingly-Known-As and her Daddipegs. The Colonel, in an attempt to comfort his daughter, mistakenly takes Clea's hand, and this gives her another idea. They will all play Guess the Hand. Clea puts Carol's hand in Harold's, which she mistakes for her fiancé's. Then she puts Brin's hand in Harold's, and Harold has no trouble identifying it. This puts Brin in the position of having to explain to Carol how Harold could identify his hand so easily.

Miss Furnival is drunk by now, and Harold takes her home. In a moment he returns, wild-eyed with rage: he has seen his apartment. He accuses Brin of being everything from a "skunky, conniving little villain" (p. 117) to a "light-fingered Lenny." Still angry from before, he attacks Brin with: "Don't tell Harold about the engagement. He's not to be trusted. He's not a friend. He's just someone to steal things from!" (p. 118). And he goes on hysterically about how he has always been a good friend to Brin, listening to all his "boring talk about women, hour after hour" (p. 118). Dramatically, he lists all of the items which have been "stolen" from his apartment, and taking his raincoat from Brin's table, breaks his most valuable antique, which the coat was hiding. While Harold and the Colonel, armed with the metal prongs from Brin's sculpture, are chasing Brin around the room, Bamberger appears, and since he sounds so much like Schuppanzigh, he is taken for the electrician. Schuppanzigh reappears through the trapdoor and thinks that the rude Englishmen are making fun of him by imitating his accent. The electrician fixes the fuse, and the stage goes black.

Unlike the other plays, *Black Comedy* is populated by stock characters—a dizzy debutante, a middle-aged spinster, a military bully, an effeminate antique dealer—and is less easily identifiable as a character study or as a play with a message than are the earlier plays. Yet it does convey a message on the theme of identity; the media for the message are the personage of Brindsley and the technique of the reversal of light and darkness. This reversal is no mere theatrical gimmick; it is necessary to the meaning of the play. The events of the entire play lead up to the moment of truth between Brin and Clea. Brin tells Clea that she had no right to ruin his chances with Carol, since it was *she* who walked out on *him:*

BRINDSLEY	*You* walked out on me. (He *joins her on the low stool.*)
CLEA	Is that what I did?
BRINDSLEY	You said you never wanted to see me again.
CLEA	I never saw you at all—how could you be walked out on? You should live in the dark, Brindsley. It's your natural element.
BRINDSLEY	Whatever that means.
CLEA	It means you don't really want to be seen. Why is that, Brindsley? Do you think if someone really saw you, they would never love you? (p. 114)

Brindsley avoids the subject, because it is too painful for him to confront. For all of his success with women, Brindsley remains basically insecure and unsure of himself. He almost marries Carol Melkett because she does not present him with confrontations or force him to face himself as Clea does; rather she flatters his ego:

CLEA	Stop pitying yourself. It's always your vice. I told you when I met you: you could either be a good artist, or a chic fake. You didn't like it, because I refused just to give you applause.
	. . . .
	Is that what *she* gives you? Twenty hours of ego-massage every day?
BRINDSLEY	At least our life together isn't the replica of the Holy Inquisition you made of ours. . . . (p. 115)

Brindsley is not the only character who is playing identity games; the farce in the play is based on mistaken identities. Miss Furnival would have the world believe that she would never let a drop of liquor pass her lips, but drink she does, when she, as Brindsley, is protected from life's revealing light; and Clea plays the part of a charwoman. Even in a play that uses stock characters, there is a relationship between the individuals in this work and others of Shaffer's dramas. Brindsley, for all his sexual bravura, is just as nervous and unsure of himself as are Bob and Clive, perhaps even more so than Clive, who makes a sincere attempt to assert his individuality and present himself honestly to the world. Carol Melkett is a paler version of Louise Harrington; both play at nicknames (Carol calls whiskey, Winnie; vodka, Vera; and gin, Ginette) and both value material things:

Then we can buy a super Georgian house and live what's laughingly known as happily ever after. I want to leave this place just as soon as we're married. . . . I don't want to live in a slum for our first couple of years—like other newlyweds. (p. 105)

Colonel Melkett, the father and figure of authority in the play, has the same doubts about Brin's future that Stanley Harrington has about Clive's: how will they make a living when their interests are the arts? The arts, then, link Brindsley with his predecessors: Clive's interest is drama, Bob's is music, Brin's is sculpture. Brindsley's identity problem—his fear of facing himself—is the "black" element in the comedy; it gives a frantic farce a serious message and helps make the play truly a Black Comedy. The themes of lying and identity link *Black Comedy* with the two following one-act plays.

IV   White Lies

As in *The Private Ear* and *The Public Eye*, there are only three characters in *White Lies:* Sophie: Baroness Lemberg, Frank, and Tom. The play takes place at Sophie's fortune-teller's parlor, a seedy living room facing the sea, on the promenade of a rundown seaside resort on the south coast of England. On the window are printed the words " '*BARONESS LEMBERG, PALMISTE. CLAIRVOYANTE.*' and in smaller letters '*CONSULTANT TO ROYALTY*' " (p. 9). It is six o'clock on a mid-September afternoon. The two most important items in the room—which shows obvious signs of poverty—are a portrait of Vassili, Sophie's former boyfriend, and a parakeet named Pericles; Sophie speaks to both of them as if they were human beings. Sophie, who is forty-eight years old, speaks with a German accent. On the evening of the play, she is talking to them of her financial problems: she has not had a client in days and has not been able to pay the rent since June. When Sophie sees that not one but two clients are waiting to see her, she is overwhelmed.

The first is Frank. He is about twenty-five years old, "cold, watchful, ambiguous." Frank is given to practical jokes and will do anything for a laugh. He has come to Sophie to arrange for her to tell his friend's fortune based on the information that Frank supplies; he wants to "stage the best joke ever played," to get Tom "so brilliantly he'd never forget it" (p. 16). Sophie is offended. She thinks of herself as a professional and maintains that she lives by the slogan "Lemberg never lies." As Frank tells the story, Tom (who is lead singer in the group called the "White Lies," which Frank manages) has taken an interest in Frank's girl friend, and Frank wants Sophie to see a tragic end for Tom if he does not leave the girl alone. Sophie will not consent to such a prostitution of her profession, but at the offer of twenty-five pounds she changes her mind, rationalizing that "it is the duty of the aristocracy to maintain itself, no matter what!" (p. 23). Frank tells Sophie Tom's history: he came from a poor working family in a mining town; his mother is dead, and his father is a drunkard who used to beat him.

After Sophie has had a few minutes to study the notes that Frank left for her, Frank returns with Tom. Unlike Frank, Tom is a "shy-looking boy of twenty-two, with a thick Cheshire accent" (p. 23). Sophie insists that Frank leave them alone if she is to achieve an accurate reading. Tom is impressed that she knows that he is a musician, but in order to establish credibility, she admits that she learned that much from Frank. She likes Tom immediately and does not want to go through with Frank's scheme, for which she has already been paid, and she claims to feel a headache on the way. As he starts to leave, she changes her mind again, either because she does not want to lose the money or because she does not want Tom to go.

Sophie tells Tom's life story just as Frank related it to her. Tom is startled and cannot believe that she could possibly be getting that information from her crystal ball. When Tom has heard as much as he cares to hear, he tells Sophie that it is all a lie: he comes from a middle-class family, with a mother who is indeed alive and a father who is an accountant. His whole present life is one enormous lie, which he invented in order to be successful in the rock-music business because "middle class is right out. No one believes you can sing with the authentic voice of the people if you're the son of an accountant" (p. 31). Sophie is stunned. She has been found out, and by a person she likes and with whom she identifies closely. Tom describes his deplorable living situation to her: he, Frank, and Helen all live in the same house, he upstairs and they downstairs. Every morning Tom has to come down and see Helen in Frank's bed, with Frank smiling at him, as Tom prepares their breakfast. Tom has never been able to tell Helen about his true identity for fear that he would lose her: "Look! Truth's the last thing she wants. She's 'in love'—that's what she calls it! She's in love with a working-class boy—even though he doesn't exist. And I'm in love with feelings I see in her eyes—and I know they don't exist. They're only what I read into them" (p. 33).

Tom's talk about love and about eyes triggers associations in Sophie's mind. She, too, was in love, with Vassili, the man in the photograph; she loved his immense black eyes. She continues to tell Tom the truth about her past. When her husband died, he left her penniless, and in order to make a living she worked as a landlady, and it was then that she met Vassili. He was a student looking for an inexpensive room; she rented one to him and was immediately attracted to him. But he had a fiancée (chosen for him by his father), whom he could not marry for another two years until he completed his studies. Sophie allowed Vassili to invite Irina to his room, and Sophie, all the while filled with hate, served them tea. One day, he revealed that he knew Sophie's secret: she was not an aristocrat, just a girl named Sophie Harburg from a poor Jewish family, and she had never been the manageress of a grand hotel, just a barmaid in a pub. She could no longer see him and advised that he marry Irina, for Sophie's sake. Before leaving her, Vassili presented Sophie with Pericles, the parakeet, as a gift. Vassili told her that Pericles was a bird of truth, in whose presence no one must ever tell a lie. Until today, she has spent her life protecting her white lies, but now she is through with them. Sophie advises Tom to go to Helen, to tell her the truth and to run off with her.

When Frank returns and Sophie tells him what happened, he demands that Sophie return his money, and when he becomes violent and throws Pericles out of the window, she does, but not until she tells his fortune: "Five of pounds: card of cruelty. Five of pounds: card of vanity. Five of pounds: card of stupidity. Five of pounds: card of fantasy. Five of pounds:—card of a loveless life. It's all in the cards, mister" (p. 42). Left alone, she stares at the photograph and tells it, "Harburg never lies" (p. 42) and discards it on the floor along with the images she had spent her life protecting.

Beginning with *White Lies* and continuing throughout the rest of his dramatic production, Shaffer's plays are developed around a conflict between two people who care for and identify with each other. Sophie and Tom have just such a relationship: they have both created false identities for themselves, and they go about life living a lie, Sophie as nobility and Tom as working-class poor.[12] Just as Walter serves as a catalyst for the members of the Harrington family, Sophie's encounter with Tom is the turning point in her life: he reminds her of her past, upsets her present, and determines her future. Her attraction to Tom is immediate: she comments first on his eyes and next on his paleness, the two aspects of Vassili to which she refers during her scene of self-revelation. She looks at him and comments on their first common trait: they are both winter people; neither one likes the sun: sunlight equals truth. Tom tells her how he likes the isolation and desolation of winter: "I went to Herne Bay last March. . . . All the sea gulls . . . looked like rows of old convalescents, huddled down in their coat collars" (pp. 25 - 26). She feels Tom's sensitivity and hears his poetic language (which approaches Clive's and Bob's) and she knows that he is one of her people; she cannot betray him for the likes of Frank. When she finally does tell his fortune, she turns it, more for his benefit than for hers. She intimates that she can no longer lie to him, and having reestablished her credibility proceeds to protect him with her white lies. She tells him that Frank's warning game was that Tom's punishment would be loneliness, not violence, and she makes him see that he is afraid of himself and not of Frank. She gives him the courage to leave Frank and his illusionary past behind and to take Helen and start an honest future; he gives her the strength to discard her pretentions and to begin facing the world as Sophie Harburg, who never has to lie again.

Tom is linked with Clive by more than their sensitivity to nature and their poetic language: they share the same kind of parents—his father has virtually nothing to do with his son and his mother belongs to the bridge set and puts on airs: "They've virtually disowned me, after all. Dad calls me 'Minstrel Boy' now every time I go home, and mother has a whole bit with her bridge club that I'm

in London 'studying' music. Studying is a better *image* than singing
in clubs. She can *see* herself as the mother of a student. Both of
them are talking about themselves, of course, not me" (pp. 31 - 32).
They are Stanley, who wants Clive to go into business, and Louise,
who will not hear of it because Clive's being in the business world is
not good enough for *her*.

Sophie's past life is also another glimpse of Louise: in her attempt
to be an aristocrat, she has to belie her heritage and denigrate
middle-class life, be it her taste in music or her weekend sightseeing
outings with Vassili:

Now *there* was a fan! He taught me everything: what groups were good,
what lousy, Top Ten, Pick of the Pops! Secretly I liked it, but it was vulgar
to admit to. After all, I was the Baroness Lemberg. His own family was just
middle class. . . . He was absolutely intoxicated by history! And because I
was an aristocrat, you see, I was supposed to know all about it. Every Sunday we went on a bus—up to Windsor Castle, down to St. Paul's Cathedral.
And what he never knew was that every Saturday night I would sit up,
secretly memorizing the facts—then speaking them next day, almost yawn-
ing, because tourism, after all, is a little common, my dear . . . [*sic*].
(p. 35)

Both Tom and Sophie are denying their pasts—she by creating a
finer image, and he by creating a lower one. Tom no longer believes
in truth, in presenting himself to the world sincerely, because
nobody does it; honesty is impossible: "Believe me, Baroness: I've
worked it out. Look—everyone makes images—*everyone*. It's like
no one can look at anyone direct. The way I see it, the whole
world's made up of images—images talking at images—that's what
makes it all so impossible" (p. 31).

Sophie feels no identification at all with Frank: he is too brutal,
too candid. He begins by asking not if she is the Baroness Lemberg,
but if she is "the witch." He insults her, bribes her, and forces her
to compromise her ideals. He also instills as much fear in her as he
has instilled in Tom and Helen. Around Frank, Sophie dwells on all
that makes her unhappy in her life—its truth. He forces her to
realize that her parlor is not filled with duchesses waiting for a
reading and that thrones are not tottered at the flip of her predic-
tions. She is no longer holding the hands of governors, princes, and
ministers of justice. She has fallen desperately since then, if ever
there indeed was any glory in her past:

Look, mister, I'm not mad, you know, there are no Duchesses out there, I know that. Just crazy spinsters, stinking of moth balls, old red men with gin in their eyes, begging me to predict just one horse race, one football pool, to make them rich for life. Rubbish people, all of them, boring me to death with their second-rate dreams. Nevertheless, I make adjustment. Other years—other tears! I spend my life now casting prophetic pearls before middle class swine." (p. 21)

While Tom and Sophie are engaged in image games with themselves and the rest of the world, Tom and Frank have a relationship based on practical jokes, a relationship that parallels Bob and Ted's in *The Private Ear*. Ted and Frank are older than Bob and Tom, have had more success with women, and take their friends under their wings—Ted seemingly instructs Bob in the facts of life, and Frank gives Tom a job as lead singer with the White Lies. The relationship between Tom and Frank is presented second-hand; that is, but for one moment when Frank brings Tom into Sophie's parlor, they are never on stage together. Their relationship parallels those of the other plays in which two men are pitted against each other in a power struggle, this time for the love of a woman who thinks she loves Frank (according to Tom) and whom Frank (according to Tom) does not even pretend to love (or to believe that such a thing as love exists at all). Sophie, Tom, and Frank all live by her adage, that "nothing is *just* anything" (p. 25); there is always another level beneath the apparent one. Sophie's adage is Shaffer's message, echoed by the characters as well as by the props.

Shaffer's two major props in *White Lies* are the parakeet Pericles and the photograph of Vassili; Pericles reminds Sophie that she is supposed to tell the truth, and the photograph accuses her (or so she imagines) of being a fraud. The photograph is really a physical representation of her conscience. In her opening monologue, she "hears" the photograph calling her a fraud and she responds: "It takes a fraud to call a fraud . . ." (pp. 12 - 13). When she is considering Frank's proposition to tell Tom's fortune, again she imagines that the photograph is accusing her, and she replies in kind: "Look, everyone cheats a little, my darling, even your Greek witches. What do you think your famous oracle at Delphi was doing?—one silly cow sitting in a lot of smoke, saying exactly what she was paid to say!" (p. 22). When she discards the photograph, she is discarding her lies, her games, her guilts, and her insecurities. She has told her last lie. Likewise, when Frank throws Pericles out of the window, she tells her first truth: as she predicted in her open-

ing monologue of the play, he is going on a long, long journey. She
is once against Sophie Harburg, and Harburg never lies.

V   The White Lies

Shaffer considers *The White Liars*, loosely based on *White Lies*, a
new play and the final version. He specifies that it should be played
before *Black Comedy* and that "the two plays represent a complete
evening's entertainment, on the theme of tricks."[13] As in *White
Lies*, the play takes place in Sophie's fortune-teller's parlor, on a
run-down amusement pier. The names of the characters are the
same, and the plot line remains very close to that of *White Lies*.
There are, however, some significant changes in the characters' personalities, in the details of Sophie's relationship with Vassi, and in
the techniques: Shaffer has eliminated the parakeet and the
photograph—at the end of *White Lies*, Pericles is sent on a long
journey, and Sophie discarded Vassi's picture—and they have been
replaced by tapes, which play Sophie's thoughts, both present and
remembered.

Frank and Tom have effectively exchanged identities from those
that they had in *White Lies*. Now Frank is shy, soft-spoken, and
gentle, and Tom is casual to the point of what Shaffer terms
"brutality." He has a heavy midlands accent and wears long hair
and bright clothes. Frank, the manager of a rock music group called
"The White Liars," wants Sophie, via her crystal ball, to warn Tom
to keep away from his girl friend, Sue. Frank tells Sophie how much
he has done for Tom: he took him out of a filthy cellar in the slums,
gave him a room in his flat, and formed a musical group for him.
After she gets over the insult of being bribed to tell a fortune, she
feels a strong identity with Frank and wants to join him in his plan
against Tom; both she and Frank are "Givers"; Tom, like Vassi, is a
"Taker," and "Takers" should be taught a lesson. Sophie divides
the whole world into the "Givers" and the "Takers": "The Givers
are the world's aristocrats. . . . The Takers are the Peasants,
emotional peasants" (p. 19).

Tom is superstitious, a great believer in fortune-tellers, and is
anxious for his reading, despite Frank's act at being disappointed by
Sophie. Sophie takes an immediate dislike to Tom, in no small
measure because he brings to Sophie's mind Vassi and the advan-
tage he took of her:

Pay the rent. "More, please!" Hellas Restaurant. "More, please!" Shop at Jaeger's, twenty pounds one jacket. Riding lessons in Richmond Park, two pounds one hour! Seats for the theatre, that boring *Elektra*—of course we must sit close to watch the faces—seventy shillings for two places, just to see bad make-up! . . . And always more. Always the same cry of More! Take and take, and take, until the cows are at home. And then what? Surprise! "Sophie, I've met this girl Irina. She's the daughter of my father's oldest friend. We are suited to each other, absolutely. We are both young. We both tell the truth. We don't pretend to be Baronesses. And so, bye-bye!" (pp. 30 - 31)

Nothing that Tom says convinces Sophie that she may be wrong about him, but he wants her to consider just three facts: he was not living in a slum, was not without money, and he had formed "The White Liars" a year before he ever met Frank. He tells of how Frank and Sue would come week after week and watch him perform. Frank pretended to be a journalist who wanted to write a story about Tom, which would mean being around him for a whole month. Frank invited Tom to move into his flat, on which he owed three months' rent, and which Tom paid. Frank, it turned out, was not a journalist at all, but an employee in a boutique on Kings Road in Chelsea, until he lost his job. Tom cannot take the responsibility of making up the lies about his past, because, as he sees it, Frank and Sue *made* him lie:

Once I'd spoken—actually spoken a lie out loud—I was theirs. They got excited, like lions after meat, sniffing about me, slavering! . . . Who was I? I didn't exist for them. I don't now! *(He rises violently.)* They want *their* Tom: not me. Tom the idol. Tom the Turn-on. Tom the Yob God, born in a slum, standing in his long-suffering maltreated skin—all tangled hair and natural instinct—to be hung by his priests in white satin! . . . Our uniform for The Liars. He designed it—she made it—I wear it." (pp. 35 - 36)

That is all that Tom can see that the "Givers" give: they give out identities and roles until the "Takers" are their emotional prisoners. Yet Sophie will not be convinced that Tom is telling the truth. Finally, he has to tell her that Frank and Sue were never lovers, and that the person that Frank really wants is Tom. When Frank returns and Tom is gone, Sophie is forced to tell Frank that Tom has left him, and Frank tells Sophie that she should not believe everything that Tom might have said about him.

Just as lies exist between Frank and Tom, so they existed between Sophie and Vassi. Five years have passed since Sophie has seen Vassi, and yet their final conversation still echoes in her ears; she still hears him telling her how it is impossible to live with liars and her replying that he should get out—words she lived to regret and tried to retract, but to no avail.

While the relationship between *White Lies* and *The White Liars* is striking, the relationship between *The White Liars* and *Black Comedy* is more subtle. Both plays examine lies and identity crises: neither Frank, nor Tom, nor Sophie can be honest about his identity; each lives in his own private world of fabricated images of himself. Only Sophie verbalizes a rationale for so deceitful a life-style: "All right, lies, so what? *So what?* So he tells a couple of—of tales just to make himself a little more important—just to shield himself a little from the sordidness of life!" (p. 33). Life is easier for her to face as the Baroness Lemberg than as Sophie Weinberg, Fraulein No-One. Tom is Sophie's reminder of Vassi; he acts on her emotions as well as on her conscience: in his presence, Sophie relives her unhappy moments as well as the guilt and suffering that her lies brought her; she thinks that Tom, as did Vassi, is calling her a fraud. Shaffer describes Tom as looking like a parakeet, the symbol which represented both Vassi and truth in *White Lies*. Tom and Brindsley share the need for adulation, for worship; Brindsley preferred the company of Carol to that of Clea because he received "ego-massage" from Carol everyday. Similarly, Frank tells Sophie that, like a Greek monster, Tom lives on worship: "He can hardly get through a day without two tablespoons of sticky golden worship poured down his throat, preferably by a girl" (p. 16). Both Tom and Vassi are represented by animals: in *White Lies*, the parakeet has the function of acting as Sophie's conscience and as a constant reminder of Vassili; in *The White Liars* the toy dog that Tom wins at the shooting gallery serves as a symbol of Tom. When Frank sees at the end of the play that Tom has left his toy in the waiting room, he realizes that it is all he has left of a former friendship. The theme of male jealousy in *Black Comedy* is echoed in *The White Liars*. Harold Gorringe would like Brindsley to spend his time and affection on him instead of "wasting" it on Clea and Carol; Frank wants Tom, and the only way to keep him in his home is by pretending to be interested in Sue.

The White Liars also shares common bonds with *The Private Ear*, *The Public Eye*, and *Five Finger Exercise*. Its link with *The Private*

Ear is the situation of two men vying for the attentions of the same woman—one man is shy and gentle, while the other is aggressive and dominant. It is related to *The Public Eye* through Frank, who takes on a role of bogus journalist and claims that he has to shadow Tom for a month and take notes on his activities for an article that he is writing. Julian assumes professional roles that do not belong to him and recommends following people around as a means of solving marital problems. There is also a common thread between *The White Liars* and *Five Finger Exercise*. Tom's mother is a reincarnation of Louise—both putting on airs and trying to recreate their children in their own images; and his father is as unimpressed with him as Stanley Harrington is with Clive. Frank exhibits the same kind of possessiveness as Louise: if he cannot have Tom, neither can Sue.

VI *Summation*

Of the five plays in this chapter, the critics were most enthusiastic about *Black Comedy*. It has been praised for its humor, originality, surprises, and grace. The only reservation that some reviews had was that the play went on too long to sustain the initial appeal of Shaffer's technique. *White Lies* and *The White Liars* received less laudatory reviews, ranging from "thin" and "stretched"[14] to "wise" and "earnest."[15] Three of the plays are dominated by intense relationships between men in competition with each other: Bob and Ted, Tom and Frank; and even Charles Sidley and Julian Cristoforou, to some extent. This battle of the wills between two men is the focal point of the plays in the next three chapters: *The Royal Hunt of the Sun*, *Shrivings*, and *Equus*.

CHAPTER 4

The Royal Hunt of the Sun

FOLLOWING a delay of six years, during which time finan-
cially cautious impresarios were reluctant to make the large
outlay necessary to stage the spectacle, *The Royal Hunt of the Sun*
was finally produced at the Chichester Festival on July 6, 1964. Its
New York debut was at the ANTA Theatre on October 26, 1965.
Shaffer has provided more background information and commentary concerning the writing of this play than for any of his other
works. He stated that, during a period of mandatory bedrest, he filled his time by reading William Prescott's classic *History of the
Conquest of Peru,* which inspired him to write *The Royal Hunt of
the Sun,* his interpretation of Pizarro's conquest of the Inca Empire.
In an introduction to the published version of the play, which he
wrote at least a year after the play had already been produced, he
set forth his intentions in writing the play, as follows:

> Why did I write *The Royal Hunt?* To make colour? Yes. To make spec-
> tacle? Yes. To make magic? Yes—if the word isn't too debased to convey
> the kind of excitement I believed could still be created out of "total"
> theatre.
> The "totality" of it was in my head for ages: not just the words, but
> jungle cries and ululations; metals and masks; the fantastic apparition of
> the pre-Columbian world. . . . I did deeply want to create, by means both
> austere and rich . . . an experience that was *entirely and only theatrical.*[1]

The themes, he wrote, were to be "an encounter between Euro-
pean hope and Indian hopelessness; between Indian faith and Euro-
pean faithlessness. I saw the active iron of Spain against the passive
feathers of Peru: the conflict of two immense and joyless powers.
The Spaniards suspected joy as being unworthy of Christ. . . . The
Conquistadors defied personal will: the Incas shunned it" (p. v).
Unlike anything else Shaffer has written, *The Royal Hunt of the
Sun* is epic in its conception and mammoth in its production. It

takes place on two continents over a period of four years, and has an emperor and a conqueror as its protagonists. The play is divided into two acts, "The Hunt" and "The Kill," with each act subdivided into twelve sections, intended solely for reference and not for indicating any pauses or breaks in the continuity of the action. The set described is that used at the Chichester Festival.

I *Plot*

When the play opens, Old Martin, the narrator, grizzled, in his mid-fifties, and dressed in the black costume of a Spanish *hidalgo* of the sixteenth century, says that he is a Spanish soldier who has spent most of his life fighting for land, treasure, and the Cross. He has been closer to Pizarro than any other man alive, and as a youth, he would have died for Pizarro, the object of his worship. The scene fades to that of a town in Spain in 1529; Pizarro enters accompanied by Hernando De Soto, his Second-in-Command, and Fray Vincente de Valverde,[2] a Dominican priest. Old Martin interrupts the action to give more background information: Pizarro had already made two trips to the New World, and now over sixty years old, he is back in Trujillo, the town of his birth, to recruit men for a third expedition. One of his recruits is the literate Young Martin, who idolizes Pizarro. Pizarro warns his men to have no illusions about the impending journey: ". . . I'm promising you swamps. A forest like the beard of the world. Sitting half-buried in earth to escape the mouths of insects. You may live for weeks on palm tree buds and soup made out of leather straps. And at night you will sleep in thick wet darkness with snakes hung over your heads like bell ropes—and black men in that blackness: men that eat each other" (p. 4). But Pizarro promises his men gold as a reward for enduring—and surviving—those hardships, more gold than they could ever imagine, and slaves who are theirs for the taking. Next, Valverde appeals to the men's religiosity: this is their chance to save the souls of heathens otherwise condemned to eternal damnation. Valverde promises that "he who helps me lift this dark man into light I absolve of all crimes he ever committed" (p. 5). Pizarro's motive is different from that of the other men: as was Arieh in "The Salt Land," he is looking for immortality, for a name that will be remembered in legends for centuries to come. He is also trying to overcome his image of an illegitimate peasant, who worked as a swineherd.

The scene quickly changes to Panama, where the soldiers of fortune are having their weapons blessed so that they might be able to
turn savages into Christians. Fray Marcos De Nizza, the Franciscan
friar on the expedition, tells the men of the noble purposes for making their trip:

You are the bringers of food to starving peoples. You go to break mercy
with them like bread, and outpour gentleness into their cups. You will lay
before them the inexhaustible table of free spirit, and invite to it all who
have dieted on terror. You will bring to all tribes the nourishment of pity.
You will sow their fields with love, and teach them to harvest the crop of it,
each yield in its season. Remember this always: we are their New World.
(p. 8)

Estete, the Royal Veedor and Overseer, is the representative of the
Crown of King Carlos the Fifth of Spain. Disagreement arises over
his position relative to that of Pizarro's: Estete professes that he
speaks with royal authority, and Pizarro recognizes no higher power
than his own on the expedition.

Pizarro doubles over with pain and explains to a concerned Young
Martin that he is still suffering from a wound inflicted on him by a
savage long ago. Pizarro tries to dispel Martin's illusions of chivalry:
a soldier's mission is to kill, no more and no less; in the army's tradition there is no glory. He advises his disciple to forget Peru and to
go back to Spain, but Martin will not leave the man who has become his idol.

To the strains of exotic music, Atahuallpa, sovereign Inca of Peru,
appears in the medallion of the sun, a second acting stage used as a
part of the play's decor. His priests warn him that Pizarro means
trouble, but Atahuallpa is determined to meet the White God.
While the Spaniards are making their way toward the Inca, they
seize one of his chiefs, who explains that Atahuallpa is the illegitimate Son of the Sun; his father had two sons and divided his
empire between them, but Atahuallpa, wanting it all, declared war
against his brother and killed him. Valverde is appalled to hear
Atahuallpa referred to as God and instructs the men to convert the
heathen Incas by any necessary methods. Again Pizarro tries to
destroy Martin's faith, this time in him: Pizarro insists that he is a
man who is not to be trusted and that Young Martin is the target for
disillusionment because he is a worshiper:

You belong to hope. To faith. To priests and pretences. To dipping flags
and ducking heads; to laying hands and licking rings; to powers and
parchments; and the whole vast stupid congregation of crowners and cross-
kissers. You're a worshipper, Martin. A groveller. You were born with feet
but you prefer your knees. It's you who make Bishops—Kings—Generals.
You trust me, I'll hurt you past believing. (pp. 17 - 18)

Later the soldiers meet the head of a thousand families who explains the Incan *modus vivendi:* in the seventh month they pick
corn; in the eighth, plow; in the ninth, sow maize; in the tenth,
mend roofs. From Atahuallpa, the Spaniards learn how Incas have
their whole lives planned for them: from the ages of nine until
twelve, they protect harvests; from twelve to eighteen, care for the
herds; from eighteen to twenty-five, serve as his warriors; at twenty-
five, marry and receive a plot of land. At fifty, all retire and live
honorably from the community. Later in the play, De Nizza attacks
the Incas' system as depriving its people of the right to
hunger—which, as he sees it, gives life meaning—as well as the
right to be unhappy:

. . . happiness has no feel for men here since they are forbidden unhappiness. They have everything in common so they have nothing to give each
other. They are part of the seasons, no more; as indistinguishable as mules,
as predictable as trees. All men are born unequal: this is a divine gift. And
want is their birthright. Where you deny this and there is no hope of any
new love; where tomorrow is abolished, and no man ever thinks 'I can
change myself', there you have the rule of Anti-Christ. (p. 52)

Pizarro thinks that his whole life may have been a path to this
day, which offers perhaps his death, perhaps new life. The hours
pass as the soldiers agonizingly wait for a messenger to summon
them to Atahuallpa. Martin spots thousands of heavily armed Incas
approaching. Before they reach Pizarro, they put down their arms
because "you don't approach gods with weapons" (p. 35). To an ex-
plosion of color and music, Atahuallpa enters and asks to see the
Spaniards' God. Valverde and De Nizza try unsuccessfully to explain Christianity to him and are enraged by what they consider his
blasphemy: Atahuallpa cannot accept the idea that a God can be
killed by men, and he calls the Pope a madman who gives away
countries that are not his; finally he casts the Bible to the ground. In
"The Mime of the Great Massacre" which follows, thousands of In-

cas are slaughtered, and Atahuallpa is led off stage at sword-point. The act ends with screams from the Indians, and a cloth of blood is drawn across the stage.

There is no break in the action between Act One, which ended with the arrest of Atahuallpa, and Act Two, much of which is composed of scenes between the two leaders. In their first conversation, Pizarro is employing the talents of Felipillo (a slim, delicate Indian, whom he captured on a previous expedition) as translator, until it becomes apparent to Martin, who understands a little of the Inca language, that Felipillo is distorting what Pizarro and Atahuallpa are saying in order to benefit his own selfish ends. In the future, Martin will learn Incan and serve as Pizarro's translator.

The priests try to explain Communion to Atahuallpa, and it sounds to him like something ridiculous, bordering on cannibalism and vampirism: "First he becomes a biscuit, and then they eat him. . . . At praying they say 'This is the body of our God.' Then they drink his blood. It is very bad. Here in my empire we do not eat men. My family forbade it many years past" (p. 49).

Atahuallpa suspects why the Spaniards have come to his land and offers to fill the room with gold in the next two months in return for Pizarro's promise to free him. De Soto cautions him about giving his word when it may not be possible to keep it, but Pizarro feels certain that Atahuallpa could never keep his part of the bargain, and so he consents. Atahuallpa orders that gold be brought in from every corner of his empire, and so "The First Gold Procession" takes place, during which the most elaborately worked objects are delivered, but not enough to fill a room; Pizarro finds Atahuallpa wanting in honesty. He reminds Atahuallpa of his promise to listen to the Christian priests; Atahuallpa has listened and thinks that they are fools. He also sees in Pizarro's eyes that the Spaniard agrees with him. Pizarro faults Atahuallpa for killing his brother and seizing the land, but Atahuallpa forces Pizarro to admit that he would have done the same thing. Pizarro mentions incidentally that sooner or later he is going to kill Atahuallpa. Nevertheless, Atahuallpa removes one of his golden earrings and hangs it on Pizarro's ear; it is the sign of a nobleman. Next, he tries to teach Pizarro one of the indigenous dances, but Pizarro's attempt at it is so funny that Martin starts laughing. Pizarro starts laughing, too, extends his hand to Atahuallpa, and they leave the stage together.

A month has passed, and De Soto returns from a reconnaissance. He reports that, for hundreds of miles, men are standing in their fields waiting for Atahuallpa, their God, to return to them. Also, in the course of the month, the men notice that Pizarro is a changed man, never before so content as now, when he spends several hours every day with the Inca. They know that Pizarro is going to find it hard to kill Atahuallpa when the time comes. As the Spaniards talk, the Incas mime "The Second Gold Procession," and the men are anxious for the division of the treasure. Only under threat of death do they disperse and postpone "The Rape of the Sun."

Just as Atahuallpa tried to teach Pizarro to dance, so Pizarro tries to teach the Inca the Spanish language and the art of fencing. Pizarro acknowledges that Atahuallpa has fulfilled his promise concerning the gold and declares Atahuallpa a free man. But his release is not so simple an issue as it appears: he must first promise that none of the Spanish soldiers will be harmed. Atahuallpa can make no such promise because he still has to avenge the death of the many men he lost at the hands of the Spaniards. Martin further complicates Pizarro's decision of whether or not to release Atahuallpa, by telling him that Atahuallpa trusts him, and that he cannot betray that trust.

After the division of the gold, there is tension and violence among the soldiers: greed has overcome them. As the men are in open conflict with each other, Pizarro continues to struggle internally. What to do with Atahuallpa? For advice, he turns to his Second-in-Command and the representatives of the Crown and of the Church. De Soto insists that Pizarro must live up to his promise and give Atahuallpa his freedom, but Pizarro is afraid that if his army is wiped out, nobody will remember his name. Pizarro feels no obligation to the king, and Estete finds Pizarro's attempt to keep a promise of life to Atahuallpa nothing more than quaint. It is Valverde's decision that "no promise to a pagan need bind a Christian. Simply think what's at stake: the lives of a hundred and seventy of the faithful. Are you going to sacrifice them for one savage?" (p. 71). From De Nizza Pizarro gets advice which he interprets to mean: "To save my own soul I must kill another man!" (p. 72). In order to protect Atahuallpa from being killed, Pizarro binds the two of them together with a rope: if the men want to kill Atahuallpa, they will have to kill Pizarro first. Atahuallpa is less concerned about his life than is Pizarro: Atahuallpa is a god and cannot be killed by a man; only his father can take his life from him. Just as Pizarro is trying to save Atahuallpa's physical life, the Inca is trying to save the Spaniard's spiritual life: "Pizarro. You will die soon and you do not believe in your God. That is why you tremble and keep no word. Believe in me. I will give you a word and fill you with joy. For you I will do a great thing. I will swallow death and spit it out of me" (p. 76).

In a hopelessly unfair trial, Atahuallpa is found guilty of killing his brother, of worshipping idols, and of having more than one wife, and he is sentenced to death by burning. Pizzaro pleads with him to accept baptism and thereby have his sentence reduced to death by strangling. He accepts, and is baptized and killed. When Atahuallpa does not regenerate his own life, Pizzaro cries out at the lifeless body: "Cheat! You've cheated me!" (p. 79) and he lies down next to Atahuallpa's body. That day, Pizarro died spiritually, and, shortly after, he died physically in a quarrel with the soldier who brought up the reinforcements. Spain brought the New World "greed, hunger and the Cross: three gifts for the civilized life. The family groups that sang on the terraces are gone. In their place slaves shuffle underground and they don't sing there. Peru is a silent country, frozen in avarice" (p. 80).

II   *Characters*

Chronologically *The Royal Hunt of the Sun* should be considered after *The Private Ear* and *The Public Eye* and before *Black Comedy, White Lies,* and *The White Liars,* but for its character studies and themes it is grouped more logically with Shaffer's last two plays, *Shrivings* and *Equus,* since the latter plays examine the theme of worship, relationships between an adolescent and a mature man, and intense relationships between two men.

A.   *Martin and Pizarro*

Young Martin worships Pizarro and relates in his opening monologue to the audience: "He was my altar, my bright image of salvation. Francisco Pizarro! Time was when I'd have died for him, or for any worship" (p. 1). The rest of the play traces the decline of this intense love and respect that Martin once felt for the Spanish hero. Martin is a fifteen-year-old orphan whom the illiterate Pizarro employs as his page because the boy can read and write. Pizarro promises Martin nothing in return for his services except disillusionment about chivalry and his noble ideals. Honor and glory for Pizarro are "dungballs. Soldiers are for killing: that's their reason"

(p. 10). Despite all of Pizarro's negativism, Martin is not discouraged and is determined to serve Pizarro, whom he calls his lord. The discomforts of traveling through the forest in the New World do not diminish Martin's reverence for Pizarro, to whom he claims to belong, to whom he can declare, "You are all I ever want to be" (p. 17). But Martin's "ever" is shortlived: he loses his respect for the *conquistador*, who fails to keep his word to Atahuallpa, a man who trusts him. This is the turning-point in Martin's life: "I went out into the night—the cold high night of the Andes, hung with stars like crystal apples—and dropped my first tears as a man. My first and last. That was my first and last worship too. Devotion never came again" (p. 63). The narration, as given by Old Martin, does not deify Pizarro, or anything else. He says that the play is about ruin; the ruin is both personal as well as national.

B. *Pizarro*

Pizarro's whole life has been a road from ruin and an attempt to find glory and thus transcend his humble origins—that of an illegitimate swineherd in a drab Spanish village—which denied him the respect of men and the love of any woman whom he could consider for marriage. He is the empty shell of a man who, like Clive and like Bob, is given to pondering the big questions in life, the kind that philosophers could never resolve: Religion, Time, Immortality. His manner of speech, however, is more rhetorical than that of his dramatic colleagues. His motivation in making another expedition to the New World is not the greed for gold (which he uses in order to entice the other men to come along), but something much deeper than any material gains: as was Charles Sidley, Pizarro is searching for the sun, for the source of life and of eternity. He sees no value in institutions such as the Court, the Military, or the Church. The sun, he believes, is worthy of worship, and for pagans he thinks that it must make a fine god, something that they can see and whose power they can experience.

Pizarro's disillusionment in life extends to women, in whom he no longer has any real interest: as everything else, women have served to be only one more disappointment in his life of shattered dreams. He blames his loss of love for women on Time, the culprit guilty of all failure in life:

I loved them with all the juice in me—but oh, the cheat in that tenderness.
What is it but a lust to own their beauty, not them, which you never can:

like trying to own the beauty of a goblet by paying for it. And even if you could it would become you and get soiled . . . *[sic]*. I'm an old man, Cavalier, I can explain nothing. What I mean is: Time whipped up the lust in me and Time purged it. I was dandled on Time's knee and made to gurgle, then put to my sleep. I've been cheated from the moment I was born because there's death in everything. (p. 32)

Pizarro almost finds the object of worship that he has been looking for when he discovers the Inca religion and meets Atahuallpa.

C.   *Pizarro and Atahuallpa*

Pizarro is a different man in Act Two after Atahuallpa becomes his fountain of new life   at least temporarily, his nihilistic attitudes and chronic pessimism diminish when he is with the Son of the Sun. There is a strong identification between the two men: both are illegitimate and both are the leaders of men. Of even greater importance is that each one considers the other a god. Atahuallpa wants to meet Pizarro in order to receive the blessing of the White God, and Pizarro finds more meaning in the Inca religion than he ever found in Christianity and comes to believe that perhaps the Incas have the answers to questions that the white man has never been able to receive: "I myself can't fix anything nearer to a thought of worship than standing at dawn and watching it [the sun] fill the world. Like the coming of something eternal, against going flesh. What a fantastic wonder that anyone on earth should dare to say: 'That's my father. My father: the sun!' . . . Since first I heard of him I've dreamed of him every night. A black king with glowing eyes, sporting the sun for a crown" (pp. 32 - 33).

During Atahuallpa's captivity, Pizarro grows closer to him than toward anyone else in life. They teach each other their respective skills (dancing and fencing) and learn to read together, like brothers. So much does Pizarro come to love and respect Atahuallpa, that he cannot let the man to whom he has promised life be killed. When finally Atahuallpa is killed, Pizarro suffers his last disillusionment in life: the Inca does not regenerate himself as Pizarro believed he would. His final attempt at worship has been yet one more disappointment.

D. *Atahuallpa*

Atahuallpa is not nearly so complex a figure as his Spanish count-erpart and functions as an antagonist rather than a protagonist. However, he shows himself to be a master of understatement when he tells his priests that the Spaniards may come to meet him because he wants them "to see [his] mountains." Thus, the soldiers suffer the perils of the Andes in "The Mime of the Great Ascent." Shaffer uses the technique of a song to show that Atahuallpa is no fool and that he understands perfectly why Pizarro and the other Spaniards have come to the Inca empire:

> You must not rob, O little finch.
> The harvest maize, O little finch.
> The trap is set, O little finch.
> To seize you quick, O little finch.
>
> Ask that black bird, O little finch.
> Nailed on a branch, O little finch.
> Where is her heart, O little finch.
> Where are her plumes, O little finch.
>
> She is cut up, O little finch.
> For stealing grain, O little finch.
> See, see the fate, O little finch.
> Of robber birds, O little finch. (p. 53)

Atahuallpa explains that this is a harvest song, and that Pizarro is the robber bird.

Unlike Pizarro's, Atahuallpa's convictions are simple and firm: his father is the Sun; he is the Son of the Sun; any human being who can be killed is not a real god. Shaffer includes details about Atahuallpa which are intended to make him a Jesus figure, such as placing his age at thirty-three. Atahuallpa and Pizarro are mutually dependent: Atahuallpa depends on Pizarro to preserve his physical life, and Atahuallpa is Pizarro's last hope for acquiring the ability to worship, a wish he tries to suppress but secretly envies in the Inca. All three characters—Martin, Pizarro, and Atahuallpa—are united by common bonds. Martin needs Pizarro for his worship, and Pizarro in turn needs Atahuallpa for his. In Pizarro's hands rests Atahuallpa's only hope for existence.

The other characters in the play have secondary roles: Valverde and De Nizza act on behalf of the Church. Hernando De Soto is at once the most practical, noble-minded, and sensitive character in the play. He regrets that Pizarro ever made a bargain with Atahuallpa, but now that he has, he expects him to honor it. De Soto cannot advise that Atahuallpa be killed after Pizarro set the conditions for his release and certainly not after he learns that the Inca trusts Pizarro. For all of the talk that the priests do about saving the souls of the Indians, only De Soto understands that the end of Christianity is love and that the means should not contradict the missionary ends in Peru.

III   Sources

Shaffer used Prescott's *History of the Conquest of Peru* as his historical source for *The Royal Hunt of the Sun* and made such changes as were necessary for his dramatic purposes. For the most part, he was faithful to history in the development of the fictionalized-historical characters and in the storyline. Francisco Pizarro was born ca. 1471 in the Spanish town of Trujillo, in the region of Extremadura. He was left as an illegitimate foundling and might have been nursed by a sow. As a boy, he worked as a swineherd and never learned to read or write. In January 1531, he left on his third and last expedition for the conquest of Peru. Shaffer is faithful also to the inclusion of the secondary characters. Prescott mentions that Pizarro was accompanied by a veedor appointed by the Crown; by Fray Valverde, who attempted to explain the Creation, the Trinity, and the Pope to Atahuallpa; by Felipillo, a malicious youth who acted as interpreter between Pizarro and Atahuallpa; and by Hernando De Soto, who, along with Hernando Pizarro (Francisco's brother), went to meet Atahuallpa as representatives of the chief of the expedition. Prescott explains that the Spaniards arrived during a period of internal strife in the Inca empire, and that the moment was right for the conquest. Conflict had arisen between the two brothers who controlled the empire, and when Atahuallpa, the more ambitious of the two, emerged victorious, he had his brother killed. The Incan emperor was an absolute despot in a totally Socialistic society and was a representative of the Sun, and there was a belief that a departed monarch would return after his death to reanimate his body on earth. (The process, however, was never believed to be so immediate as Pizarro expected from Atahuallpa.) Prescott is not so specific as Shaffer concerning the number of Incas who were slaughtered, but puts the number at between 2,000 and 10,000. Atahuallpa was not led off by the soldiers at sword-point, but rather by Pizarro himself, and without any violence; Pizarro considered the emperor as a guarantor of his own safety. Pizarro assured him that in the Spanish camp he would be received as a friend and a brother. Prescott estimates Atahuallpa's age at about thirty, which Shaffer interprets as thirty-three in order to sustain his Atahuallpa/Jesus identification.

Atahuallpa was astute enough to realize that the Spaniards had not come to the New World just to save souls and offered them a room full of gold and a smaller room filled twice with silver. The soldiers took his promise as idle boasting in an attempt to gain his freedom. The Spaniards of authority agreed that the most expedient way of disposing of the problem was considered just, and that to set him free was considered too dangerous an act. Atahuallpa was found guilty on twelve charges including usurpation of the crown, assassination of his brother, idolatry, adultery, and insurrection against the Spaniards (the last being the most important charge in the trial). A mere four paragraphs of Prescott's monumental work mention the friendship that the Inca extended to Pizarro and of Pizarro's visible emotion when Atahuallpa pleaded for his life.[3] Pizarro's first concern, however, had to be for his men. On August 29, 1533, Atahuallpa was taken to the town square in chains. Just as Atahuallpa was to be burned, Fray Valverde promised him that if he accepted Christianity, his penalty would be reduced to death by strangulation, and thus he was executed. Historically, Pizarro did not die quite so soon after Atahuallpa as he does in the play. It was not until June 26, 1541, that a band of Almagro's men (whose leader Pizarro had executed in 1538 and whose lands he denied them) attacked and murdered him. The spectacle, too, has its origins in Prescott: he describes the soldiers' painful ascent of the Andes; the procession of the Incas and of Atahuallpa, royally attired; the decorations made from the plumes of tropical birds; and the gold processions bearing the largest booty in history.

Some critics find Shaffer's source of inspiration in Antonin Artaud's "La Conquête du Mexique,"[4] an outline of which appeared in published form in 1950.[5] Artaud describes his work of "Theater of Cruelty" as the struggle of Christianity against primitive religion and the question of racial superiority. He mentions such details as music, dance and pantomime, poetic lamentations, and philosophical discussions, all of which appear in *The Royal Hunt of the Sun*.

IV *Critical Appraisal and Interpretation*

Reviewers were more sharply divided over *The Royal Hunt of the Sun* than over any other of Shaffer's plays. Writing in the *New York World Tribune and The Sun,* Norman Nadel praised the symmetry of poetry, the noble speech and strong wisdom, and placed Shaffer in the highest rank of twentieth-century British playwrights: "No Englishman in the century, save Shaw and Christopher Fry, has achieved such sensible beauty with words, such noble clarity of ideas. *The Royal Hunt of the Sun* might well be a masterpiece."[6] The *Saturday Review*[7] called it the season's most thrilling, imaginative, and beautiful event, and *America*[8] called it the finest play of the season. The *New York Daily News*[9] praised Shaffer's use of language in this beautiful play. Peter Coe[10] praised *The Royal Hunt of the Sun* as a towering event of theater and literature, and Martin Esslin[11] echoed Coe's respect for the text of the play. Other critics had good words to say about Shaffer and his work, but found this play to be overwritten, overscrutinized, and too long.[12] Many critics praised Shaffer's daring and the vitality that he put back into the theater.[13] Those who criticized the play found the script to be heavy and self-conscious,[14] of "bloated form, pretentious theme, mundane prose and sentimental sermonizing,"[15] and a play that, for its lack of characters and language, has a hole in the middle that the spectacle cannot conceal.[16] Howard Taubman reconciled the critical excesses when he stated that the play was first hailed as a masterpiece and later condemned as a showy fraud, and that the truth is somewhere between those extremes.[17] Stanley Richards saw fit to include it in *Best Plays of the Sixties.*[18]

To criticize *The Royal Hunt of the Sun* as being empty, as lacking in characters or themes, is unjustified; Shaffer accomplished all that he intended in the play. The themes are big, perhaps grandiose, the characters are heroic, and the *mise-en-scène* is formidable. The criticism of the language is only slightly more justifiable. The language is grand, but in its attempt to be poetic as well as profound it sometimes loses the quality of spontaneity that characterizes the speech of Clive Harrington, for example. But if Pizarro's language seems to lack lyricism, then De Nizza's poetic speech more than compensates for it. *The Royal Hunt of the Sun* may not be judged on literary criteria: it was Shaffer's purpose to create a work of "total theater" for the stage and not a piece of dramatic literature for the printed page.

As for Shaffer's comments on the play, in one statement he said: "Ultimately, the play is about a man's search for immortality."[19] And in another article, Shaffer called it "a play about two men: one of them is an atheist, and the other is a god. . . . The relationship . . . is intense, involved and obscure, between these two men, one of whom is the other's prisoner. . . . They are mirror-images of each other. And the theme which lies behind their relationship is the search for God, the search for a definition of the idea of God. In fact, the play is an attempt to define the concept of God."[20]

With *The Royal Hunt of the Sun*, Shaffer brought to the stage all of the spectacle that had been in his imagination for a long time. In addition, he developed themes contained originally in his television script "The Salt Land." It brought to life the Peru of the Incas, a land that in fact was "a natural gold mine," an expression used by Jo to describe the land of Israel. It gave another treatment of the epic theme of the settling of the New World. It developed the idea of worship and man's need for God as well as that of the search for immortality which obsesses both Arieh and Pizarro, as it did such great thinkers as the Spanish philosopher Miguel de Unamuno. Thus, in one sense, *The Royal Hunt of the Sun* completed work that Shaffer had begun earlier; in another sense, it was a precursor of his portrayal of the intense struggles between two men, which dominates *Shrivings*, and tells of the death of a god, which is one of the themes of *Equus*.

CHAPTER 5

Shrivings

IN a note written in 1974 for the published version of *Shrivings*, Shaffer stated that this play is a substantially rewritten version of *The Battle of Shrivings*, which opened at the Lyric Theatre in London on February 5, 1970, to mixed reviews from the critics.[1] The play is the result of dual sources of inspiration: Mahatma Gandhi's decision to renounce sex, which he considered a source of aggression, and the student protests of the 1960s, which grew out of the Vietnam War and the killings at Kent State University. For Shaffer, it is his "American play," which he associates with his sojourns in 1968 and 1969 in New York, then plagued by violent confrontations between Flower Children and constructions workers. The play, in its published form, has never been produced.

Shrivings is Shaffer's only three-act play, and it is divided into five scenes. Just as is *Five Finger Exercise*, it is true to the spirit of the classical unities: it transpires during a single weekend, treats a single problem, and takes place in a house called Shrivings, in the Cotswold Hills of England. Like the house in *Five Finger Exercise*, there is a multi-level set with the living room, study, and kitchen on the lower level and the bedrooms on the upper level. The atmosphere is one of tranquility and dedication, as in the original medieval Shrivings, a house of retreat, confession, and penance.

I *Plot*

The play begins at five o'clock on a Friday afternoon, and without any preliminaries, the story starts with the first speech, as Lois Neal, Sir Gideon Petrie's secretary, answers the telephone and tells the person on the other end that Sir Gideon will stage a peace vigil by sitting in Parliament Square on Saturday and Sunday to protest the production of all arms in the United Kingdom. This weekend, the house is closed to travelers in anticipation of the arrival of Mark Askelon, a noted poet and former student of Gideon. On Monday, Mark and Gideon are going to receive awards for letters, Gideon for the publication of his twenty-fifth book on philosophical *Explorations* and Mark for the publication of his *Collected Poems.* Gideon is excited about Mark's expected arrival, and he wants everything to be perfect for him. Rather than being excited, Mark's son, David, who lives at Shrivings, is apprehensive about receiving his father, whom he has not seen in six years. Gideon reminds David that life has not been easy for his father since his wife's death, and that perhaps Mark is coming to Shrivings because he needs both of them.

Mark, a relic of the man he used to be, has a less-than-spectacular arrival. From the moment he enters Shrivings, he begins to fulfill his intention of making himself unwelcome, and he surprises Shrivings in a manner for which no one in the house is prepared. He criticizes Lois's vegetarianism; he calls Shrivings a "Commune for Transients"; he questions Lois's adulation of Gideon; and he ridicules the Peace Movement with rank insensitivity. But he receives a surprise, too: his son has left Cambridge University and has devoted himself to making furniture in Gideon's home. (Since Mark does not read letters, he never knew the news about David's life.) Mark is disappointed, but makes light of the situation by calling carpentry the only profession with "an indisputable patron saint!"[2] David's latest piece is a chair, almost a throne, for Gideon, and Mark is more than a little jealous. Gideon alarms Mark by describing the vigil that will take place. First Mark reacts by attacking the question of nonviolence. He asks Lois, Gideon, and David what they would do if an attacker with a weapon were to threaten one of them. Then he goes beyond all bounds of decency in describing his insensitivity during a riot in New York in which he saw young protesters being mercilessly beaten by gangs of construction workers, all of which he claims to have watched uncritically as he sipped martinis. Having upset the household sufficiently for his first afternoon, Mark retreats to his room and prays to the ashes of his dead wife to keep Gideon, David, and Lois safe from him, while at the same time he decides to become, metaphorically, the attacker, with his tongue as his weapon.

It is 10:30 at night in the second scene. Mark, half-drunk in his room, alternately tries to blame David ("master carpenter to Gideon Petrie," p. 143) and alternately blames himself for getting carried away for the sake of "one pretentious American slit" (p. 143).

Downstairs, as David rolls marijuana for a smoke, Lois admonishes him for not having warned her in advance of his father's character. David would like to smash a plate and have it represent his father. Lois rebuffs David's attempt to steal a kiss, which for her would violate the spirit of Gideon's renunciation of sexual activities. She also decides for David that he will attend the peace vigil, for which Gideon thinks a two-day hunger strike will add pathos to the situation. Lois suggests fasting for everyone who plans to attend. Mark proposes that for all the love they claim to feel, he can make Shrivings reject him in just one weekend; Gideon insists that that could never happen. Mark confesses that he *wants* to be proven wrong and agrees that if Shrivings can survive a weekend of him with its gentleness intact, he will return to Sir Gideon's humanitarian fold. If not, it is really Gideon and his philosophy that lose, and the philosopher must never preach improvability again. Mark begs Gideon to save him. He was not so unfeeling as he said at the Wall Street demonstration; in fact, he was so upset that he vomited down the side of the building. He also admits to having murdered his wife but offers no details. The Battle of Shrivings has begun.

Act Two begins on Saturday night, after the first day of the vigil. Mark listens over the radio to the report on the demonstration, and Gideon, David, and Lois return home, intoxicated with the vigil's success. In defiance of the hunger strike, Mark has prepared himself "the very smallest repast" (p. 160) of lamb chops, salad, roll, and wine, and, to Lois's horror, David accepts his father's invitation to join him. After a six-year absence, Mark sits down to talk with his son, and, because of the jealousy that he feels for David's relationship with Gideon and his guilt at having alienated himself from David, Mark thinks that David is trying to tell him to mind his own business when he asks about his son's plans for the future. Lois questions Mark's motives for coming to Shrivings; she used to admire him as a poet, but now she has lost all of her respect for him and finds him contemptible.

At this point, Mark wants to adapt an experiment in which total strangers were asked to inflict electric shock on innocent victims. He designates four apples as representing various degrees of punishment, from mild pain to death, and given license to say anything he would like, he attempts to provoke so much anger against him that he will be asked to leave the house. To bring the experiment to its conclusion, he reveals "secrets" about Gideon's sex life, even accusing him of stealing David, his own friend's son, to satisfy his sexual appetite for young boys. David picks up the death apple and smashes it over and over again. Mark returns to his room in repentance, and ends the scene by throwing brandy in the face of the statue on his late wife's shrine.

In the second scene of Act Two, it is ten o'clock in the morning following what has been a bad night for all. Lois is furious with David because he pressed the death apple, and thereby did exactly what Mark wanted. For David, it was worthwhile to lose Mark's Apple Game because it "stopped the voice." Gideon tries to convince Lois that they must smother Mark with acceptance. Despite Mark's allegations that Gideon is a homosexual, Gideon maintains that he gave up sex with his wife because he considered it the main source of aggression in himself; his wife found the decision too rigorous for her and she left him. David wants to protect Gideon from the impending harm to him: he knows his father and wants Gideon's permission to ask him to leave Shrivings. Gideon is now alone in his resolution that Mark must stay. Meanwhile, Mark is planning to thicken the plot by bedding Lois, and with charm and cunning he does just that.

Act Three takes place following the Sunday afternoon vigil, which Lois missed while she was in bed with Mark. Mark is eager for Lois to get downstairs so that their secret might be revealed to David and Gideon. He becomes adamant, and she realizes that the sex act was just one more move in his game to enrage Gideon. Mark hints broadly to Gideon and David at what was going on in his room while they were at the demonstration. Gideon is appalled that Mark, even within the context of the battle, could have stooped so low.

Mark, who has tried to win the battle by using first Gideon, and then Lois, finally uses his own son. In a last effort to turn David against Gideon, he advises Gideon that it is no longer necessary to withhold the secret of David's origins, and he assails his son: "Look at you! Is that my face? Dirty olive out of the standard wop jar! Is that my body? Slack-waisted camel-walk: the harbour hump! Get with it, you lump of Italy—it took a lot of pasta to make you!" (p. 198). David asks that Gideon stop the voice, and Gideon in return only wrings his hands. David can stand no more of the philosopher's passivity and lashes out against him: "Theories and hopes and vigils and fasts! And *nothing! Lovely nothing!*" (p. 200). He ends by howling at his former idol to "FUCK OFF!" David rushes out of the room, and Mark congratulates Gideon on his victory; he acknowledges that Gideon has won the Battle of Shrivings, even if (as he alleges) it meant torturing an innocent boy in the process. Gideon faints, and Lois tries to revive and encourage him to eat, and then in a tirade against him she tells him that he is a phony. In the climactic scene, he betrays his philosophy of nonviolence and strikes her.

In his room, Mark tries to make David believe that he was lying about his son's supposed illegitimacy so that he would not have to tell him how he killed Giulia, the boy's mother. One night, as his wife lay crippled in bed, Mark brought another woman into their room and had sex with her right in front of his wife. Three weeks later, Giulia died. Mark, David, Gideon, and Lois are four lost souls: Lois does not know where she is; Mark has nowhere to go in life; Gideon has just one word for Mark, "Dust"; David stretches out his arms to Lois, but she remains motionless and expressionless, as the light fades.

II *Characters*

The types of the estranged father, the abandoned son, and the reluctant young woman first appeared in "The Prodigal Father." Here they appear in fuller form. Mark is a troubled man. The manifestations of his problems are cruelty, jealousy, and alcoholism; the root is guilt, for the death of his wife, for his estrangement from his son, and for disappointment in himself. Mark and Giulia's marriage was one more in a series of bad unions in Shaffer's plays. At the core of the marital problems, there was mutual canonizing between husband and wife which, ironically for Mark, led to an ambiguous love-hate relationship. The marital problems of Mark and Giulia were far deeper than those of the Harringtons, in part because Mark was an atheist who "wrote about Catholicism like it was a disease" (p. 124), and Giulia, devoutly religious, was forced to read her devotional books in secret. Unlike Belinda's shortlived idealization of Charles Sidley, Giulia's adoration of her husband endured to the end. After her death, Mark regarded Giulia as a saint, much as she revered him during her lifetime. Mark loved Giulia intensely, and his love was so profound that it produced a change in his poetry: he gave up his biting criticism of the Catholic Church to sing of his love for his wife. Strangely enough, the resentment that Mark came to feel for his wife was an outgrowth of the love and admiration that she felt for him, and of which he never considered himself worthy.

Mark's plan at Shrivings is to divide and conquer, to turn Gideon, David, and Lois against one another and thereby destroy Gideon's ideas on the perfectability of man; to prove that "the Gospel According to Saint Gideon is a lie. That we as men cannot alter for the better in any particular that matters. That we are totally and forever unimproveable" (p. 156). In fact, Mark wants to *lose* the verbal battle that he declares against Gideon, because Mark needs him; he needs to have Gideon win him back to the Humanist philosophy and not let him stumble into the arms of Mother Church. The battle that Mark initiates against Gideon, then, is really a manifestation of his own internal struggle.

Mark is and always has been a joyless man. Life has never held the excitement and passion for him that it offers to other people. He confesses to Lois how desperate and jealous his lack of passion has made him: "I was never quite alive. . . . Inside me, from my first day on earth, was a cancer. An incapacity for Immediate Life. When I was a boy, the crowd at football matches jumped to its feet, shouting. All I could see was a ball and legs. At student dances, I hopped in silence. . . . . The only music I ever heard was words, and the clear thought of Gideon Petrie" (pp. 189 - 90). Joy never came to him even as an adult, and the lack of it turned to poison in him and made him hate the people who *could* feel it, the people whom he envied, including his wife and his son: "When you were six, I watched you race your bike through the olive trees. Your mother was standing beside me. Your mouth opened with glee. Hers too. All I got were the mouths opening and shutting. No glee. Just physical movements. I stood there hating you both" (p. 203).

Mark also suffers from an identity crisis; neither does he know who he is, nor can he identify with his heritage. He goes about the world as a spiritually dead Christian; yet like Sophie's in *White Lies* and *The White Liars*, his heritage is Jewish. He also believes that David is lost because he never knew either a home or a homeland: "We are not Place People, David or I. My father was not called Askelon, but Ashkenazy. Israel Ashkenazy, of the ghetto face. He bequeathed me no home on earth: only envy of home in others. That boy will never walk a Dorset lane like an Englishman—rock a Vermont porch like a Yankee—doze under a Corfu cypress like a Greek. He's a mongrel! Russo-Jewish-English-Neopolitan! Whelped in one island, weaned in another" (p. 152).

In several respects, Mark's situation is similar to Pizarro's. Just as Pizarro tried to drive the admiration of him out of Young Martin, so Mark proved to Giulia how undeserving he was of her love. Also like Pizarro, he lashes out against worshipers in general, while secretly a need of something to worship engulfs him. Furthermore, he condemns the Church and all that it represents as he goes through life in search of an ideal worthy of him. Like Pizarro, he, too, is attempting to immortalize his name: Pizarro did it through his conquest of Peru; Mark is trying to do it through his poetry. And Mark and Pizarro are both joyless, empty men. He is also like Arieh in "The Salt Land," both of whom thirst for a homeland.

David is the only issue of Mark's union with Giulia and the most disturbed son in any of Shaffer's plays before *Equus*. (David speaks in "Wows" and expresses his emotions in shrugs.) He grew up with ambiguous feelings toward his parents. There is no indication that he did not love his mother while she was alive, but after her passing he speaks of her with a total lack of feeling or respect. In words strikingly similar to those of Walter to Clive in *Five Finger Exercise*, Lois reminds David that he owes respect to Giulia, who, after all, was his mother, and he replies: "Once. Since then, Father immortalized her in poetry. Now she belongs wholly to Penguin Books" (p. 125). He suffers from a complete lack of self-confidence, and he talks of how he has nothing to offer the world: "I can't give anybody anything. Sometimes I think all the opposite things I feel should just cancel me out, and make me invisible" (p. 127). David lacks Clive's poetic approach to life and his understanding—or at least a sincere attempt at an understanding—of his problems. His thoughts are concerned with getting from day to day and gratifying his immediate physical desires, principally through smoking marijuana. His talents are manual, and he finds creative escape in carpentry.

As a son abandoned by his father, David more nearly approximates Jed, the son in "The Prodigal Father," than any of Shaffer's other dramatic creations. He grew up away from his father and for a six-year period received no communication from him except telegrams that said that it was still inconvenient for him to return home. When finally Mark attempts to communicate with his son, he assumes that David's curious manner of expression is a brusque way of telling him that he has lost the right to ask personal questions.

In the absence of any other father-figure, David has adopted

Gideon—or allowed Gideon to adopt him—as his only family. It is again the Young Martin - Pizarro relationship of a young boy over-come with admiration for the man he idolizes, until disillusionment turns him irrevocably against the object of his reverence. Gideon's is apparently the only friendship and love of which David can feel secure: his mother (a former ballerina, who used to dance him to sleep) is dead; his father estranged himself from him long ago; there are no lovers or other friends in his life. In Gideon, David has found a substitute for the relationships that his life lacks. Gideon is his sur-rogate father who encourages David's interest in carpentry—and is handsomely rewarded in return. David's finest work is the chair, which Mark labels "The Chair of Paternal Wisdom," for the "First Pope of Reason." David saved the chair to present to Gideon on the day of Mark's arrival, perhaps to show off his masterwork, or perhaps, as Mark suspects, to demonstrate that the bestowal of such a gift has to be earned.

David does not share his father's reputation for success with women. There is no mention of girls in David's past, and his present consists of half-hearted attempts to win the attention of Lois, six years his senior, uninterested in the young man, and repelled by the very thought of sex. Mark is as strongly opposed to his son's behavior as Stanley is toward Clive's. He reveals his displeasure and jealousy by intimating on the one hand that David and Gideon are lovers, and on the other that David and his whole pot-smoking generation "can't get it up to save [their] stoned lives!" (p. 197). He speaks, too, of how Giulia could not stand her son: "Even in her, deep down, was the natural Italian horror of the Unmale" (p. 197). In part, to prove to David that he is sexually superior to both a nineteen-year-old and to Gideon (whom Mark insists "is completely queer"), Mark feels compelled to seduce Lois, and becomes the first man ever to have sex with her. David passively accepts whatever Lois tells him to believe. He is too bewildered with the absence of a past in his life to be concerned with the present, much less the future. David never knew a real home before Shrivings, and the concept, even the word *home*, is sacred to him. As Mark envies the ability to feel emotion, David envies the quality of inner peace, and when his father asks what he would really like to be, he says that he wants to experience the serenity of an old woman whom he once met.

Lois, the pretty American secretary, had her personality shaped by a strict Catholic upbringing, and she demonstrates the disastrous constraints that zealous religion in childhood can have on an adult's sexual attitudes. She describes her childhood to Gideon and David: "D'you know the last thing *I'd* see at night when I was a kid? A beautiful plastic Jesus, like the ones they have in taxis to prevent crashes, only bigger. It had these great ruby tears on its face, and I'd have to pray to it before turning out the light: 'Dear Lord, make me a Good Catholic and a Good American. Amen!' " (p. 127). David makes two attempts to kiss Lois. On the first occasion she turns away coolly, and on his second attempt she "*lets herself be kissed, but remains inert*" (p. 145). Mark accuses her of living with Gideon because with him she is safe from sex and free to make the meals and the rules without ever losing her virginity. He is appalled by her hypocrisy: "Forever a Vestal Vigin *[sic]*. . .! Sagging Jesus, protect me from all Liberal American Virgins!" (p. 177).

In addition to proving that he is more of a man than either David or Gideon, Mark takes Lois to bed in order to raise the level of hostility in the house against him. The experience is not spectacular for either of them; Mark found Lois to be as "cold as haddock. . . . Deep Freeze Dora, the Tundra Gash!" (p. 197), and for Lois it was "just a fat old man, dropping his sweat on me!" (p. 207). Lois is Mark's double: she does not know what enjoyment is, either.

Gideon's excessive passivism, coupled with Mark's antagonism, cause Lois to rebel against her former mentor. Mark is successful in convincing Lois that Gideon is a phony, and she is quick and hard in repeating those ideas to Gideon in the final scene of the play. While Mark is trying to reconcile his relationship with David, Lois is downstairs ending hers with Gideon: "Do you know what a phoney is, Giddy? . . . Someone who says Peace because there's no war in him. I don't mean he drove it out—I mean he never had it. It's easy to be chaste when you've got no cock, Giddy. . . . No wonder she left you, your wife. No wonder she just got out, poor stupid Enid. She found out what a phoney she was hitched to" (p. 208).

Mark's former professor and once the object of Lois's and David's worship is Sir Gideon Petrie, author, philosopher, and President of the World League of Peace. He is a hybrid of Mahatma Gandhi and Bertrand Russell and the mouthpiece of the Humanist philosophy, which he embraces. Most of the information about his past life is revealed by Mark in tirades designed to make Gideon angry enough to ask him to leave Shrivings. It is not a personal hatred of either Gideon or his philosophy that motivates him to humiliate the professor, but rather jealousy of the love and respect that he has won from Mark's son and a displaced self-hate brought on by the death of his wife and the loss of his son. The battle between Mark and Gideon is philosophical. Is Gideon's self-proclaimed pacifism so highly developed as to overcome any attack that Mark might make on him and his two disciples? Mark asks Gideon to justify his attitude given the most extreme case, that of Hitler, and Gideon maintains that "the evil you do fight you enlarge. . . . You arm yourself to destroy gas chambers in Poland. Five years later, you are melting the eyeballs of fishermen on the Yellow Sea. We've had centuries of fighting back for Freedom and Justice. It doesn't work" (p. 138). When Mark can make no inroads against Gideon's goodness by using remote examples, he decides to attack the man personally in front of his two disciples. Since Gideon renounced sex with his former wife, Mark considers this to be the vulnerable area, which for Gideon will be indefensible:

Why do you imagine, Miss Neal, that your employer gave up sex? Because he found you ladies such a block on his path to virtue? Don't you know the only sex Gideon ever really enjoyed was with boys? Slim brown boys with sloping shoulders. He used to chase them all over Italy on our walking tours. And then, of course, the guilt would chase him: and I'd have to endure boring vows of repentance all the next day—to be broken again, naturally, all the next night, in the very next piazza! In the end he gave everything up. Guilt, nothing but guilt! The world saw only a Great Renunciation on the grandest philosophic grounds: but not so Enid. All she saw was a self-accusing pederast, pretending to be Ghandi! (p. 177)

Gideon feels compelled to defend himself, or at least to explain himself, to his Owl (David) and his Falcon (Lois). David protests that homosexuality is a boring subject, but once Gideon begins to speak, David sits on the floor to enjoy the talk:

When I was young, I had, as they say, sex on the brain. I meant by that, that even when I worked on equations, or read Political Science, the impulse of my attention was somehow sexual. Sex was everywhere. A girl's hair bobbing down the street. The sudden fur of a boy's neck. The twitching lope of a red setter dog. In flowers, even—the smell of cow parsley in a field of poppies would almost make me faint. To say I was bisexual would have been a ludicrous understatement. I was tri-sexual. Quadri. Quinti. Sexi-sexual, you might say! (p. 182)

Although there is more reason to believe Gideon than Mark, the subject of Gideon's sexual preferences remains ambiguous.

The names of the three men are of biblical origin and are rich in symbolic value. Mark was a first-century Jew who took a Roman name and who authored the earliest of the four Gospels. Likewise, Mark Askelon's heritage is Jewish, but he goes through life oblivious to his past, living an atheistic present, and toying with the idea of returning to Mother Church (either Roman or Greek) in the future. His last name is derived from Ashkelon, one of the five major cities of Philistia, and his actions bear out the biblical associations of the Philistines. Gideon's name is that of a tribal leader in Israel who defeated the Midianites in the twelfth century B.C. and who was offered the kingship of Israel but refused it because only the Almighty is Israel's King. Just as the biblical Gideon overcame a Philistine people, so the dramatic Gideon wins the Battle of Shrivings, even if it means losing everything else in the process. David's name has the Hebrew meaning of the Beloved, and beloved he is to both Mark and Gideon, but his character is antithetical to that of the biblical soldier and king. He is not the heroic David slaying Goliath, nor the majestic, marble David that Michelangelo sculpted, but rather more the innocent, childlike David of the bronze statue by Donatello. Perhaps the only trait that he shares with his biblical namesake is that of being morally irresponsible.

III   Themes

The play is as much concerned with exposition on philosophical questions for which Gideon and Mark are spokesmen as it is with plot and character development. Some of the questions are constants in Shaffer's theater; others appear for the first time. The basis of the play is the conflict between aggression and passivism—the aggression represented by Mark, and the passivism by Gideon. The very core and pride of Gideon's life is his philosophy of non-violence; as President of the World League of Peace, he is its foremost proponent. He believes in peaceful demonstrations—vigils and fasts—rather than in violent revolution. He carries his philosophical ideas to the extreme in refusing to defend a person who is dear to him against an attacker, since that would reduce him to the level of the ruffian. His belief is that Man is good and that his nature is improvable to the point of near-perfection. His only objection to the philosophy of the Flower Children is their desire for oneness with Nature, which is aggressive: "The Drug Children of today cry: "Unite with Nature!' I say: Resist her. Spit out the anger in your daddy's sperm! The bile in your mother's milk! The more you starve out aggression, the more you will begin yourselves!" (p. 148). He objects to sex because he sees it as the major stumbling block to people's peace with each other; for him it is a separating rather than a unifying act:

This supreme experience of union appeared to me with more and more force each time, to be simply a twin act of masturbation, accompanied by murmurs designed to disguise the fact. . . . I grew to hate the very shape of desire. Its parody of closeness. Its separating climax. Finally, I came to know that for me, it was the main source of aggression. That before I could even start on my innocence, I would have to give it up. (p. 183)

The institutions that were attacked by Pizarro in *The Royal Hunt of the Sun*—and then some—are further attacked by Gideon. The smallest unit is that of the family. Shrivings, he insists, is "not a family, as so many people know it—a box of boredom for man and wife—a torture chamber for the children. That idea of family must soon be obsolete, surely?—a miserable little group, marked off by a flat door, or a garden fence!" (p. 152). Gideon believes that home is not the place given by birth, but the place taken by adoption: "Country can be a mental prison, and patriotism an ape's adrenalin" (p. 137). He also assails materialism, patriotism, and, of course, religion: "Mangerism, or worship of Family; Flaggism, or worship of Tribe; Thingism, or worship of Money. In our theatres and on our screens, we have taught you to find the act of killing men exciting, and the act of creating them obscene. You can go to Church, and respect the stopped mind. You can go to the war memorials, and respect the stopped body. What more do you want?" (p. 147). His strongest statements are those on man's alterability, the area in which he and Mark are most at odds: "If we know *one thing* about Man, it is that he cannot *stop* altering—that's his condition! He is unique on earth in that he has *no* fixed behavior patterns! . . . There is no proof whatever that man is born inherently aggressive" (pp. 170 - 71).

Mark agrees with Gideon in his criticism of social institutions. In a speech which calls to mind those of Pizarro, he denigrates the flag-worshipers and shows how something that begins as innocently as good citizenship can become uncritical allegiance; and the clergy, who start by making laws, eventually destroy individuality. Mark can feel only contempt for "the insane Popes! The Rabbis of Repression!" (p. 190). He sees no glory in Europe's past, no shining heritage for the young to honor, no heroes for them to worship; just doom, death, and destruction. He advises Lois at the beginning of the last act that the best thing she can do is return to the United States and leave Europe behind: ". . . Everything bad started here. The pox. The subjugation of woolly heads. The social layer cake, which God's hand alone is allowed to crumble. Above all, the Police State. That's our main gift to the world. We've never been without it" (p. 191). And again, in words much like Pizarro's, he curses "the kneelers! The followers of carriage axles. The motorcade boys. The smart saluters" (p. 191). The only ideals that Mark once held were Gideon's: he, too, believed that man could be better than he is, but he lost his faith the day of the Wall Street riots; he lost the faith he had and discovered no other with which to replace it.

Mark confesses that life as he is living it can never be happy for him. He needs something in which to believe because he is Man, and Man needs to live with a dream: "I wish I was an animal, and could live without a dream. I wish I was a child, and could live in a Church. But I'm a man, and I've known you [Gideon]. Where else can I go?" (p. 210). Gideon sees the root of all of Mark's problems in his pessimism: "Smugness! The endless smugness of pessimism! Under all that litany of woe I heard only one note: *relish!* Comfort in the idea of your own perpetual failure" (p. 169).

Just as are Mark and Gideon, Lois, too, is in favor of people and opposed to labels:

I believe in the people, yes. And I believe that most of them don't want any part of the world they've been given. They don't want war. Or politics. Or organised religion. They've been taught to want these things by the ruling class, just desperate to keep its power. If they could ever get their heads straight, ordinary people would realise what history is all about. How it's just the story of a great big lie factory, where we're [*sic*] all been made to work every day, printing up labels: Serf. Heretic. Catholic. Communist. Middle-class. And when we're through, we're made to paste them over each other till the original person disappears, and nobody knows who the hell he is any more! (p. 165)

IV   *Summation*

The characters of *Shrivings* are already evident in the radio script "The Prodigal Father" and even earlier in "The Salt Land." The situation is that of a father and son who have been estranged throughout the formative years of the son's development, and consequently they are strangers to each other when finally they meet at the mansions that are Glenister and Shrivings. Mark bears resemblance to any number of characters in previous plays of Shaffer. His function is something like that of Walter in *Five Finger Exercise:* the stranger who comes into a family situation and leaves it forever changed. He also assumes the role of Ted in *The Private Ear,* in his sexual competitiveness: Ted against his friend Bob; Mark against his friend Gideon. He shares characteristics with Stanley and Bob from the same two plays: like Stanley, he is a father out of touch with his son; and like Bob, he has to admit that he could never dominate a woman (despite his reputation as a sexual athlete). He is similar to Pizarro in his lack of faith in organized religion. He characterizes the Old and New Testaments as: "vengeful Daddy, wrapped in clouds," and "Mobile Mary, whizzing up to Heaven" (p. 169). He suffers the same disappointment in his son as the fathers in "The Prodigal Father, "The Salt Land," *Five Finger Exercise, White Lies,* and *The White Liars.* Finally, just as with Jed and Leander and Clive and Stanley, the indication at the end of the play is that father and son have reached some temporary reconciliation. The joylessness of Mark's life makes him both a descendant of Pizarro and a forerunner of Dr. Dysart in *Equus.*

David shares traits of the young men in "The Prodigal Son," *Five Finger Exercise,* and *The Royal Hunt of the Sun,* as well as Alan in *Equus.* He is the rejected son, just as is Jed, but unlike Jed he is not bitter toward his father. Indeed, like Clive Harrington, he wants very much to get along with his father and is willing to go further than Clive in his pursuit of a relationship with him. Clive is willing to agree with his father only to the point that he does not contradict his mother or side with him against her. David is willing to reject Gideon's fast and to defy Lois's rules of vegetarianism for Shrivings by eating during the two-day fast—and lamb chops at that. David's needs are the same as those of Young Martin: both need someone to love and respect. For Young Martin it is a conquering hero; for David, a renowned philosopher.

Lois had two idols: Mark for his forceful poetry and (like David) Gideon for his gentle philosophy. She shares with Pizarro a loss of faith in Catholicism. (She loves Mark's anti-Catholic collection of poems *Wafers of Death.*) And, like Young Martin, before the end of the play Lois loses her respect for her two heroes. She shares an intimate bond with Lucy in "The Prodigal Father," not so much as an individual as in her relationship to other characters: Lois had a repressive, Catholic rearing imposed by her parents; Lucy is an orphan who lives under the suppression imposed by Lady Sylvia Glenister.

Gideon is the play's philosopher and bears a strong resemblance to De Nizza, who speaks of spreading love in the midst of a crowd bent on killing and looting. He resembles Pizarro in his speeches which blast the flag-wavers and cross-kissers. Mark introduces the question of Gideon's sexuality, a question which concerns Clive, Frank *(The White Liars)*, Harold Gorringe *(Black Comedy)*, and later Alan in *Equus*. His marriage, which ended in divorce, was as problematic as those of the Harringtons, the Sidleys, Arieh and Kulli Mayers, and also of the Askelons.

The theme of lying and the technique of game-playing in *Shrivings* have their origins in earlier plays. Lies dominate the plot of *Five Finger Exercise, White Lies, The White Liars, Black Comedy,* and *The Royal Hunt of the Sun.* (In "The Salt Land," too, Arieh is willing to agree to help Jo in the future as repayment for a favor in the present, knowing that he may very well break his word to his brother.) The pivotal point of the play is the Apple Game, similar to but more drastic than the games that Tom and Frank *(White Lies* and *The White Liars)* are accustomed to playing with each other. (No less a precedent are the games that Clea plays with everybody else in the room in *Black Comedy.*) A final technique that deserves mention is the effective use of overlapping dialogues in the last act, conversations that take place among characters who are on two different levels of the stage (a staging device already used in *The Royal Hunt of the Sun*). There is a sequence of Mark and David's conversation, then a sequence of Gideon and Lois's. Each builds to its own climax, while each complements the other.

The short run of the original *The Battle of Shrivings* and the lack of a staging of the revised *Shrivings* suggest that this play does not merit its own chapter. But it does: the characters, themes, techniques, and stagecraft serve as a transition between *The Royal Hunt of the Sun* and Shaffer's most recent play, *Equus*.

CHAPTER 6

Equus

E QUUS is, to date, Peter Shaffer's crowning dramatic achievement, his most widely acclaimed play, by critics and public alike. As such, it is fitting to have it occupy the final chapter of the body of this study. It is the culmination of the characters, themes, preoccupations, and techniques in all of the plays that precede it. The play was first presented in London by the National Theatre at the Old Vic on July 26, 1973, and opened in New York at the Plymouth Theatre on October 24, 1974. However, to focus on just the London and New York successes of *Equus* is to do Mr. Shaffer an injustice; the play has enjoyed runs in every corner of the globe, and has made theatrical history in Spain by ending the taboo of nudity on the Spanish stage. The story is based on an event that a friend of the playwright related to him. One night in a stable in Britain, a boy from a "Thou-shalt-not family" blinded twenty-six horses. Shaffer never confirmed the event, and the man who told him of the incident died before Shaffer could learn any more about the case. The story fascinated him, and he had to write his own interpretation of the tragedy. The event is historical; the treatment that it receives in the play is fictitious and bears the Shaffer trademark.

Just as is *The Royal Hunt of the Sun*, *Equus* is a play in two acts, subdivided into scenes (twenty-one in Act One and fourteen in Act Two), and the action is continuous. The changes of scene indicate a change of time, place, or mood. A substantial portion of the play is information presented through flashbacks, in this mystery which examines an adolescent's past for clues that would motivate the commission of his bizarre crime. The principal action of the play is set in the Rokeby Psychiatric Hospital in Southern England; the time is the present. The production that Shaffer describes in the text is that which was directed by John Dexter (who also directed *Black Comedy* and *The Royal Hunt of the Sun*) at the National Theatre.

I *Plot*

As the play opens, in silence and darkness, Alan Strang is fond-
ling a horse's head, and the horse is nuzzling his neck. Dr. Martin
Dysart, a child psychiatrist, breaks the silence with a monologue.
He is troubled about the horse, not about the boy, and he confesses
that he is lost in asking questions that are unanswerable. He begins
his narration with the day that Hesther Salomon, a magistrate,
came to beg him to accept Alan as a patient. Only after hours of
pleading the case could she persuade a court to allow the boy to
enter a psychiatric hospital rather than be put into prison for life,
and she is convinced that Dysart is the only man within a hundred
miles who can help him. (She feels the "vibrations.") Dysart finds a
fascination in the case, and, despite the fact that he is overworked,
accepts the new patient. At his first session with Dysart, Alan is
silent except for the television jingles that he sings in response to
the doctor's questions. Dysart concludes that at least one of Alan's
parents forbids him to watch television. When the nurse comes to
take Alan to his room, he is reluctant to leave Dysart's office, and as
he exits he passes "dangerously close" to the psychiatrist. Dysart's
fascination grows. Like Alan, the doctor has been having nightmares, and he blames them on Hesther for having brought Alan to
him. Dysart achieves his first breakthrough with Alan: the patient is
now speaking and tells Dysart that his father forbids him to watch
television, a prohibition which Alan's mother considers extreme.

In order to assess clearly the parents' religious attitudes, Dysart decides to pay the Strangs a visit on a Sunday. Frank Strang is
still at work (Sundays are nothing special to him), and Dora Strang
tells the doctor that Alan was always especially fond of horses. As a
child he had her read to him over and over again the story of a talking horse called Prince, which only one boy could ride. Alan also
learned by heart the passage about horses in the Book of Job. Alan
loved the word *equitation* and savored the word *equus,* the only
word he had ever encountered with a double "u."[1] Mrs. Strang also
tells the psychiatrist that hers was always a "horsey family." Frank
gets the doctor alone to fill him in on some information that he considers significant and that he is certain his wife did not mention.
Frank blames Alan's problems on his mother's reading to him night
after night biblical passages about the death of Jesus. For Frank, it
is all just so much "bad sex." What little instruction Alan has about

sex, he received from his mother, who linked sex to love and love to God.

Dysart must find out about Alan's screams of "Ek" in the night, but Alan will only answer Dysart's questions if the doctor answers his, one each in turns. Dysart needs to know what was Alan's first memory of a horse in his life; Alan especially wants to know if Dysart is married. When Dysart dismisses the boy for reverting to singing television jingles instead of answering the question, Alan sullenly tells of his first experience at the age of six with a horse. A horseman let Alan join him on Trojan and ride as fast as he liked. His parents saw him, became worried, and caused Alan to fall. Alan claims that that was the last time he ever rode. To make it easier for Alan to release further details to him, Dysart gives the boy a tape recorder. Alan calls the technique stupid, but takes the machine nonetheless.

In three unexpected visits, Dysart acquires a wealth of information about Alan. Mrs. Strang pays a call on the doctor and tells him that when her husband tore an exceptionally objectional religious picture from the wall over Alan's bed, her son put in the same place one of a horse, photographed head on, that appeared to be all eyes. Dysart's next visit is from Mr. Dalton, the owner of the stables at which Alan blinded the horses. Dalton reveals that Alan was introduced to the stables by a young woman named Jill Mason. Although Alan never admitted it, Dalton suspected that he was riding secretly at night. And so he was, because "it was *sexy*" (p. 47). Finally, Mr. Strang appears with information that he was embarrassed to convey in his wife's presence. One night he caught Alan reciting a parody of a biblical genealogy and then kneeling in front of the photograph of the horse, and beating himself with a coat hanger. Before leaving, Frank tells Dr. Dysart to ask Alan about the girl he was with on the night he blinded the horses. Frank refuses to say any more.

In their next conversation, Dysart asks Alan how he found the job at the stables and how Jill instructed him in the grooming of horses. Alan remembers how he loved touching the horses, but goes into a rage when Dysart wants to know about Jill: he accuses him of being a "Bloody Nosey Parker! Just like Dad" (p. 57). It is Alan's turn to ask the questions, and he wants to know if Dysart has sex with his wife; it is Alan's guess that Dysart never touches her. Dysart orders Alan out of his office and has to admit to himself that Alan has pinpointed the psychiatrist's "area of maximum-vulnerability" (p. 59). Dysart uses Hesther's shoulder to cry on as he relates the details of his sterile marriage. She reminds Dysart that it is his job to return Alan to normality, but Dysart is not certain that he considers it a blessing to be "normal."

Dysart's techniques of getting Alan to talk have become more and more sophisticated: first answering questions in turn, then using a tape recorder, and now playing a game called Blink, through which he hypnotizes Alan and gets him to talk in detail of his naked midnight rides on Equus. The rides begin as religious rituals and end in masturbation. This poetic and overpowering scene ends Act One with a blackout.

Act Two begins with another one of Dysart's monologues; it begins with the same sentence that he used to begin the first act: "With one particular horse, called Nugget, he embraces" (p. 74). Again he asks rhetorical questions regarding his profession and his position within it. While he is speaking, the nurse rushes in to report a terrible scene that has just taken place between Alan and his mother. Mrs. Strang brought her son his lunch; he threw it at her, and she slapped him. Dysart orders her out of the room. She tries to explain what she has been going through as a mother, and that anything that Alan has done is a result of what *he* is and not anything that his parents have done to him. This is Dysart's first indication that Alan resents not only Frank, but Dora, too. Alan denies anything he said under hypnosis, while at the same time suggesting that he would take a truth drug, which will "make" him say things that he is withholding. Dysart confesses to Hesther that he is reluctant to cure Alan if it means taking away his worship, the very core of the boy's life. Furthermore, he envies Alan for having the passion that is missing in his own life. Hesther believes that in Dysart Alan has found a new god, or at least a new father.

Alan is repentant and sends the doctor a note with an apology for having denied what he said under hypnosis, and further he acknowledges that he knows why he is in the hospital. Dysart is elated and sends for Alan for a session in the dead of night. He gives him an aspirin and lets him believe that it is the truth pill, and Alan begins to speak freely. He likes the consulting room and finds it hard to believe that Dysart would give up his job as Nosey Parker in order to move to a place where the old gods used to live before they died. Alan also has difficulty believing that gods die. He lets it "just slip out" that he knows the extent of his doctor's unhappiness. Alan requests that Dysart ask him a question, just to see if the pill has had its effect yet; Dysart wastes no time in asking about Jill Mason. One night after work, Jill started talking to Alan; she told him what beautiful eyes he had and that she had noticed him looking into Nugget's eyes "for ages." She suspected that, like herself, Alan found horses, and especially their eyes, sexy. She knew that Alan no more enjoyed going back to his home than she enjoyed returning to hers, and she invited him to go to a skin flick with her. When Alan saw in the film a nude woman for the first time, he was transfixed. Then suddenly he noticed his father in the audience. Frank caught his son watching a "dirty" movie, but what was worse, Alan caught his father. Mr. Strang insisted that he was at the theater on a business matter with the manager, and Jill assured him that it was her idea and not Alan's that they go to the film. Alan refused to go home with his father, insisting that it was proper that he see the young lady home first. Alan realized then that his father is just another man like all others; he also realized that he wanted to be with Jill—he wanted to see her breasts, just as he saw the breasts of the woman in the film. When Jill suggested that they go off together, Alan eagerly accepted. She took him to the stables, and they both undressed, but every time Alan touched Jill, he felt horsehide; when he tried to kiss her, he "heard" Equus disapproving; when he tried to make love to her, he was impotent. In a rage, he ordered her out of the stable, took a metal pick and with it put out the eyes of six horses. Then, left alone and naked, he begged to be found and killed.

The play ends with Dysart's final monologue, his strongest indictment of the work that he is doing: he will not only relieve Alan of his pain, he will relieve him of all feeling. The play ends where it began, with Dr. Dysart feeling that he is as much a slave as is a horse: "There is now, in my mouth, this sharp chain. And it never comes out" (p. 106).

II *Characters*

The play is the story of Dr. Martin Dysart, a talented child psychiatrist in his mid-forties. Unlike Clive Harrington, Mark Askelon, and Bob *(The Private Ear)*, Dysart is not known to the reader through the opinions of the other characters; he is revealed exclusively through his own words, often spoken in extended monologues similar to those of Shaffer's Pizarro. Dysart's speeches are much like those of Pizarro and of De Nizza: Pizarro's laments are personal, but the implications are religious and philosophical; De Nizza's contradict conventional thought and contain unexpected twists, which shock the audience.[2] The opening monologues of both the first and second acts are startling speeches: on seeing a boy and a horse in tender embrace, Dysart's concern is not for the boy, but rather for the horse, another way of saying that he is concerned about himself.

Throughout the play, he insists on an identification between himself and the horse. He sees the horse as "nudging through the metal some desire absolutely irrelevant to filling its belly or propagating its own kind. What desire could that be? Not to be a horse any longer? Not to remain reined up for ever in those particular genetic strings?" (p. 17). And that is Dysart's problem exactly: "I'm wearing that horse's head myself. That's the feeling. All reined up in old language and old assumptions, straining to jump clean-hoofed on to a whole new track of being that I only suspect is there" (p. 18). He acknowledges that the questions that he asks should remain unspoken, unthought: they are not only useless, they are subversive. They strike at the very heart of his life's work and convince him that what he is doing clinically is wrong ethically.

Dysart is suffering from a *malaise* both personal and professional, one which he prefers to call "professional menopause." The problem is that Dysart has lost faith in what he is doing—he no longer thinks that eliminating individual passions and restoring his patients to normality is a service to them. He even doubts that he *knows* what he is doing: "In an ultimate sense I cannot know what I do in this place—yet I do ultimate things. Essentially I cannot know what I do—yet I do essential things. Irreversible, terminal things. I stand in the dark with a pick in my hand, striking at heads!" (p. 106).

The head at which he is currently striking is that of Alan Strang, the adolescent boy who blinded six horses. Dysart's reaction to this case is his strongest ever, not because he is horrified, but because he envies Alan; he wishes that he could know the kind of passion that brought his patient to that savage act. Alan and Dysart both have private passions and fantasies: Alan's consists of ritualistically riding Equus, his god, once every three weeks; Dysart's passion is for the ancient Greek civilization, about which he spends night after night reading books and looking at photographs. He cannot resist contrasting his impotent attempts at recapturing the Greek civilization with Alan's wild midnight rides:

Such wild return: I make to the womb of civilization. Three weeks a year in the Peleponnese [*sic*], every bed booked in advance, every meal paid for by vouchers, cautious jaunts in hired Fiats, suitcase crammed with Kao-Pectate! Such a fantastic surrender to the primitive. And I use that word endlessly: "primitive." "Oh, the primitive world," I say. "What instinctual truths were lost with it!" And while I sit there, baiting a poor unimaginative woman [his wife] with the word, that freaky boy tries to conjure the reality! I sit looking at pages of centaurs trampling the soil of Argos—and outside my window he is trying to *become one*, in a Hampshire field! . . . Then in the morning, I put away my books on the cultural shelf, close up the kodachrome snaps of Mount Olympus, touch my reproduction statue of Dionysus for luck—and go off the hospital to treat him for insanity. (p. 81)

Dysart's marriage surpasses in its sterility all of the other empty unions in Shaffer's plays. For all of Alan's pain and suffering, Dysart envies him because he experiences, expresses, and receives emotion. Dysart says of his own wife: ". . . If you're kinky for Nothern Hygenic [*sic*] as I am, you can't find anything more compelling than a Scottish Lady Dentist. . . . I see us in our wedding photo: Doctor and Doctor Mac Brisk. We were brisk in our wooing, brisk in our wedding, brisk in our disappointment" (p. 60). Dysart would like to believe that his wife has caused their barren marriage—that it is her fault for sitting and knitting for other people's children night after night, as he admires the classical world via photographs. But it is untrue: "I imply that we can't have children: but actually, it's only me. I had myself tested behind her back. The lowest sperm count you could find" (p. 81). As much as passion, as much as knowing worship, Dysart craves someone unbrisk, whom he can take to Greece and instruct: he wants a son. In his bitterness, in his rationalization, he makes himself believe that, if they did have a son, he would turn out as passionless as his mother.

Since he accepted Alan Strang as a patient, Dr. Dysart has been having a nightmare, which serves as a microcosm of his problem. He is chief priest in Homeric Greece, and his job is that of cutting the insides out of young children and offering them up as sacrifices to the gods. He has two assistants, and he is afraid that one day they will notice that behind his mask he is green with nausea over his task. If they ever discover his secret, he will be the next victim. On every child on whom Dysart is supposed to perform the sacrifice, he sees the face of Alan Strang. Alan's stare, Dysart imagines, is accusing him: Alan lives his passions; Dysart does not.

Alan, the lean seventeen-year-old boy, is Shaffer's most troubled character. He exists nearly outside of society; as Dysart puts it, "He can hardly read. He knows no physics or engineering to make the world real for him. No paintings to show him how others have enjoyed it. No music except television jingles. No history except tales from a desperate mother. No friends to give him a joke, or make him know himself more moderately. He's a modern citizen for whom society doesn't exist" (p. 79). In order to fill the void in his life, Alan depends on an object of love and worship. As a child, he spent night after night with his mother reading from the Bible, and thus he developed a religious worship. He never learned anything about the essence of Christianity or about the message of Jesus; his fascination was for the violence of the march to Calvary. Instead of a peaceful Jesus illuminated from within, Alan had over his bed a picture that even his mother has to admit was ". . . a little extreme. The Christ was loaded down with chains, and the centurions were really laying on the stripes" (p. 44). When his father tore it down, Alan replaced it with a picture of a horse, which emerged as the new object of his worship.

The first picture had a masochistic effect on Alan. One night, when Alan was supposed to have been asleep, Frank passed his room and heard his son reciting a parody of biblical genealogies, in which the Jesus/horse identification is obvious: "Prince begat Prance. . . . And Prance begat Prankus! And Prankus begat Flankus! Flankus begat Spankus. And Spankus begat Spunkus the Great, who lived three score years! . . . (kneeling) And Legwus begat Neckwus. And Neckwus begat Fleckwus, the King of Spit. And Fleckwus spoke out of his chinkle-chankle! . . . And he said 'Behold—I give you Equus, my only begotten son!' " (pp. 49 - 50). The biblical influence is clear; the names that Alan chose are associated with the experiences that he had had with horses. Prince is the horse in the storybook that he enjoyed as a child. The Neckwus and the Flankus are the parts of the horse with which his body comes in contact. The Spit catches Alan's attention when he sees it coming from the horse's mouth. The Spankus is what he is doing to himself while he recites the genealogy: he beats himself with a wooden coat hanger.[3]

Alan's beliefs about horses are based on elements from the Old and New Testaments. Equus, like Jesus, is in chains for the sins of the world, and he lives in all horses. In turn, for taking him out of his chains, Equus promises Alan salvation by making the two of them into one: horse and rider shall be one beast—the kind of being that the South American Indians considered to be a god until a rider fell from his animal. Alan went into Equus's stable—that is, his Holy of Holies—to wash and brush him, and he "heard" the horse say that he should mount and ride him. The first time, it was ride or fall—that is the Straw Law. (Equus was born in the straw.) The preparations for his ride every three weeks were religious rituals that he performed for his god. First Alan put on Equus's sandals, sandals of majesty, made of sack. Next he put on the chinkle-chankle—the reins: Equus did not like it ". . . but he takes it for my sake. He bends for me. He stretches forth his neck to it" (p. 68). Then Alan took Equus to his place of Ha Ha, his field, and withdrew from the Ark of the Manbit, the stick that he put into his own mouth. It was a sacred stick for him, and he used it during every ride: "So's it won't happen too quick" (p. 70). Then Alan touched Equus all over, as one would touch a lover: "Everywhere. Belly. Ribs. His ribs are of ivory. Of great value! . . . His flank is cool. His nostrils open for me. His eyes shine. They can see in the dark . . . Eyes!—" (p. 70). Finally he gave Equus his Last Supper, a lump of sugar, which Equus accepted as a sin offering. At last, he was ready to mount his god! Equus's naked hide against Alan's naked skin hurt the boy: "Knives in his skin! Little knives—all inside my legs" (p. 71).

The horse was not only the object of his worship, but also his invitation to freedom and the source of his sexual release. Alone and naked at midnight on Equus, Alan freed both himself and his horse from society's restrictions. Together they rode against their foes: the Hosts of Philco—the electrical appliances that Alan sold at the shop—and the Hosts of Jodhpur—the clothes with which horses are adorned for shows. The speech that Alan recited during his ritualistic-orgasmic rides is fraught with historical, religious, and sexual implications. His rides began as invocation and ended in orgasm:

And Equus the Mighty rose against All!
His enemies scatter, his enemies fall!
TURN!
Trample them, trample them,
Trample them, trample them,
TURN!
TURN!!
TURN!!!

The Equus noise increases in volume.
(shouting) WEE! . . . WA! . . . WONDERFUL! . . .
I'm stiff! Stiff in the wind!
My mane, stiff in the wind!
My flanks! *My* hooves!
Mane on my legs, on my flanks, like whips!
Raw!
Raw!
I'm raw! Raw!
Feel me on you! *On* you! *On* you! *On* you!
I want to be *in* you!
I want to BE you forever and ever!—
Equus, I love you!
Now!—
Bear me away!
Make us One Person!
   He rides Equus frantically.
One Person! One Person! One Person! One Person!
   He rises up on the horse's back, and calls like a trumpet.
Ha-HA! . . . Ha-HA! . . . Ha-HA!
   The trumpet turns to great cries.
HA-HA! HA-HA! HA-HA! HA-HA! . . . HA! . . . HA! . . .
HAAAAA!
   He twists like a flame.
   Silence.
   The turning square comes to a stop in the same position it
   occupied at the opening of the Act.
   Slowly the boy drops off the horse on to the ground.
   He lowers his head and kisses Nugget's hoof.
   Finally he flings back his head and cries up to him:
AMEN!
   Nugget snorts, once. (pp. 72 - 73)

From his mother, whose word he respected, Alan learned that there
is a progression from sex to love to God. It was natural, then, for
him to turn the object of his worship into the object of his sexual attraction.[4] His mother also taught him that God knows and sees
everything.

   Alan's blinding of the horses was brought about as a result of suffering three disappointments in rapid succession, and not just by his
impotence with Jill. First, he saw his father at a pornographic
cinema. Then he realized that his mother was the cause of his
father's having to go to such a place. Finally, he experienced
failure, brought on by the religion that his mother had taught him.

The impotence was Alan's final shame. He warned Jill never to tell anyone, and even tries to hide the truth from Dr. Dysart. Over and over again he insists that: "I put it in her! . . . All the way! . . . I shoved it. I put it in her all the way" (p. 100). But Dysart knows better; he knows that if Alan had been sexually successful with Jill, he would have had no cause to blind the horses. Alan's reason for the blindings were two: first, Equus "saw" him in his moment of failure and disgrace; second, he turned away from Equus, and like the Greek gods, Equus is jealous and vengeful. Alan knew that Equus would never allow him to be successful with a woman. Hiding the pick behind his back, Alan approached Equus gently: "Equus . . . Noble Equus . . . Faithful and True . . . Godslave . . . Thou—God—Seest—NOTHING!" (p. 103).

Martin Dysart and Alan Strang individually are well-drawn characters, both presented with deep penetration into their motivations; even more profound is their relationship with and mutual effect upon each other. Many of the play's finest scenes take place between Alan and Dysart in his office, described in the stage directions as having the appearance of a railed boxing ring. The vibrations of which Hesther spoke are apparent from their first scene together. Dysart immediately identifies that one or both of Alan's parents forbade him to watch television. From the first, Dysart is affected by Alan to the point of having nightmares, and Alan found the man whom he could trust. The fact of the nightmares shows how Alan and Dysart mirror each other. In their subsequent encounters, Alan proves that he is every bit as astute as the doctor. When the psychiatrist asks Alan if he has a special dream, Alan returns the question to him. Unlike Alan, Dysart answers it: "Carving up children" (p. 36). His truthful answer gets the first smile out of Alan. Alan's initial question is whether Dysart is married and the next is if his wife is a doctor, too. And Dysart knows perfectly well how to handle Alan: when to let him stew in his own anxiety; when, at the first sign of regression (more television jingles), to dismiss him from the office. The threat of having to leave Dysart's office and not unburden himself is enough to make Alan talk—even about horses.

Much like those in *Shrivings*, the characters in *Equus* have the double function of serving as human beings with individual preoccupations as well as acting as mouthpieces for philosophies and ideologies. There is the classical struggle between Apollo, the Greek god of healing and medicine, of morality and ethics, and Dionysus, the god of fertility, for whom the worship was ecstatic and orgiastic, and whose enemies seemed to be turned into animals and were driven mad. Alan's interest in Dysart extends beyond the man's professional capacity of a psychiatrist and into the realm of his private life. Alan's concern is Dysart's marriage. He knows that a special bond exists between the doctor and himself, and that Dysart, therefore, cannot be enjoying a good marriage. He also wants to know if the Dysarts have children. If they do, Dysart is not the sexual failure that Alan is; also it will be that much more difficult for him to be emotionally adopted by Dysart.

For Alan, Dysart has become his new object of reverence. Equus was a destructive god and led Alan to a criminal act; Dysart is helpful and is trying to relieve him of his pain. In his first monologue, Dysart establishes an identification between himself and a horse. Alan has established a relationship between the horse and a god. When Dysart takes away Alan's old god, which Alan is ready to give up, the boy has to be able to replace it with a new one, and so his new object of respect becomes Dysart. Alan and Dysart share a mutual dependency (as did Pizarro and Atahuallpa): Alan is looking, if not for a god to worship, at least for a father to love and respect. Dysart is looking for a son, someone whom he can instruct. The facts that Dysart has come to grow so close to Alan, that he has come to doubt the value of his profession, that he envies the level of raw passion and instinct on which Alan lives, make him reluctant to cure his patient. Alan *knows* worship and *acts* upon it; Dysart can only read and think about it. He is jealous, and he does not want to take away the one thing that gives focus to Alan's life: "Without worship you shrink, it's as brutal as that. . . . *[sic]* I shrank my *own* life. No one can do it for you. I settled for being pallid and provincial, out of my own eternal timidity. . . . I watch that woman [his wife] knitting, night after night—a woman I haven't *kissed* in six years—and he stands in the dark for an hour, sucking the sweat off his God's hairy cheek!" (p. 81).

Dysart is only too aware of what curing Alan will do to him: it will make him "normal." He will never again blind a horse (or do anything else with one, either); he will no longer be tormented by nightmares of Equus, but at what cost? Dysart has promised Alan that he can take away the nightmares, but in another monologue he confesses what price Alan will have to pay for that relief: "When Equus leaves—if he leaves at all—it will be with your intestines in his teeth. And I don't stock replacements" (p. 105). Later, to the audience, he expands on how much of a disservice he is doing to Alan by curing him:

I'll take away his Field of Ha Ha, and give him Normal places for his ecstasy—multi-lane highways driven through the guts of cities, extinguishing Place altogether, *even the idea of Place!* He'll trot on his metal pony tamely through the concrete evening—and one thing I promise you: he will never touch hide again! With any luck his private parts will come to feel as plastic to him as the products of the factory to which he will almost certainly be sent. Who knows? He may even come to find sex funny. Smirky funny. Bit of grunt funny. Trampled and furtive and entirely in control. Hopefully, he'll feel nothing at his fork but Approved Flesh. *I doubt, however, with much passion!* . . . *[sic]* Passion, you see, can be destroyed by a doctor. It cannot be created. (pp. 105 - 106)

Dysart has been living a life devoid of any real passion and he wants Alan to escape the same fate. However, professional considerations prevail, and he has begun the process that might turn Alan into one more unfeeling, normal member of society, one who will never know ecstasy again. Dysart will turn Alan into a man who one day might marry and thereby be reduced to his own unfeeling level.

Frank and Dora Strang's marriage is not so stormy as that of the Harringtons, but it does have one seemingly insurmountable problem: she is devoutly religious, and he is an atheist. Thus, Frank holds his wife responsible for Alan's condition and for his crime. As he sees it, religion is the root of the problem. Against her husband's wishes, Dora has spent much time reading to Alan from the Bible, and in Frank's opinion that reading could lead to nothing but trouble:

A boy spends night after night having this stuff read into him: an innocent man tortured to death—thorns driven into his head—nails into his hands—a spear jammed through his ribs. It can mark anyone for life, that kind of thing. I'm not joking. The boy was absolutely fascinated by all that. He was always mooning over religious pictures. I mean real kinky ones, if you receive my meaning. . . . Call it what you like. All that stuff to me is just bad sex. (pp. 33 - 34)

In addition, he is opposed to Alan's watching television, formerly Alan's only pleasure in life. Frank resents, too, that his wife did not respect his wishes and allowed Alan, unbeknown to him, to steal off to the neighbor's house to watch television. More than the programs *per se,* he resented the conspiracy that existed between his wife and his son, whom he feels has been stolen away from him. He has to admit that Alan has always been closer to his mother than to him, and in keeping with his nature, Frank was never able to talk to his son about sex, and any knowledge that Alan has, he gained from his mother's point of view.

Dora defends her marriage, the family atmosphere, and the way that she and Frank reared their child. She blames Alan's actions on the devil:

We've done nothing wrong. We loved Alan. We gave him the best love we could. All right, we quarrel sometimes—all parents quarrel—we always make it up. My husband is a good man. He's an upright man, religion or no religion. He cares for his home, for the world, and for his boy. Alan had love and care and treats, and as much fun as any boy in the world. . . . Whatever's happened has happened *because of Alan.* Alan is himself. Every soul is itself. If you added up everything we ever did to him, from his first day on earth to this, you wouldn't find why he did this terrible thing—because that's him: not just all of our things added up. . . . I know only he was my little Alan, and then the Devil came. (p. 77)

Dora's reasoning about Alan's being himself is no mere rationalization; it is her sincere belief, and one that appears also in Clive's highly poetic speech on individuality to his father in *Five Finger Exercise.* What is unconvincing is her sudden about-face to blame Alan's problem on the devil. If Dora's ideas on her son's individuality are to be taken as correct, they contradict Dysart's theory that Alan's condition is the result of all of his experiences with horses, with his parents, with religion, and with sex: "Moments snap together like magnets, forging a chain of shackles. Why? I can trace them. I can even, with time, pull them apart again. But why at the start they were ever magnetized at all—just those particular moments of experience and no others—I don't know. *And nor does anyone else"* (p. 75). Dysart believes in Alan's individuality and in his right to keep it, yet he proceeds to add the "moments of experience" together and then to take them apart, in order, so to speak, to defuse Alan's problem. It is apparent from his concluding monologue that he endorses Dora's ideas, that Alan is Alan, but he has to deny his heart, follow his head, and cure the boy, and thereby he reduces Alan to his own level of reason over instinct, a trait which he so much dislikes in himself. In the opening monologues of the play, Dysart asks rhetorically, "Is it possible, at certain moments we cannot imagine, a horse can add its sufferings together—the non-stop jerks and jabs that are its daily life—and turn them into grief?" (p. 17). In the opening monologue of the second act, Dysart asks a similar question about Alan and thus establishes an identity between Alan and the horse; he now establishes the link between himself and his patient.

As Dora stated, Alan did know security in his parents' home until he suffered the disillusionment of finding his father at a pornographic movie theater. Despite the prohibitions that Frank placed on Alan, and even despite his low opinion of his son's aptitudes, Alan had a basic respect for him. He even quotes him to Dr. Dysart: "Who said 'Religion is the opium of the people'?" (p. 28), which Alan took to be original with his father. Alan's former image of his father and subsequent disillusionment are what Jung would call *enkekalymmenos,* a phenomenon in which what a child considered to be a true image of his parents is destroyed, when, for one reason or another, the veil is lifted from the child's eyes and he sees his parents as they really are.

Catching his father as he did was not entirely bad for Alan: it improved his self-image and showed him that even the most upright people have secret lives. It showed him that he and his father are not really so different after all: "I suddenly thought—*They all do it! All of them!* . . . *[sic]* They're not just Dads—They're people with pricks! . . . *[sic]* And Dad—he's just not Dad either. He's a man with a prick too. You know, I'd never thought about it" (p. 94). So Alan had a clearer picture of his father. For all of Frank's raving at the ill effects of watching mindless television programs and his insistence on the importance of reading to improve the mind, he is just a man. For the first time, too, Alan saw his mother in a new light as a wife: "She doesn't give him anything. . . . She likes Ladies and Gentlemen" (p. 94), and Ladies and Gentlemen are never naked. Alan is forced to reevaluate his parents, and his sympathy now rests with his father: "Poor old sod, that's what I felt—he's just like me! He hates ladies and gents just like me! Posh things—and la-di-da. He goes off by himself at night, and does his own secret thing which no one'll know about, just like me! There's no difference—he's just the same as me—just the same!—" (p. 95). The realization that all men "do it," including his father, gave Alan license to accept Jill's suggestion that they go off together for sex.

The remaining characters in the play are Jill Mason, Harry Dalton, Horseman/Nugget, Hesther Salomon, and a nurse, the last of whom requires no comment. Jill Mason is hardly individualized: she is a young woman who is necessary to introduce Alan to the world of heterosexuality and thus bring about his failure, his shame, and finally his crime. Harry Dalton, the owner of the stables, represents the voice of society: Alan is a criminal and should be behind bars, not in a hospital at the taxpayers' expense. Significantly enough, the same actor portrays both the Horseman on Trojan and Nugget, the "horse" that Alan rides at the end of Act One. Having the same actor play both roles establishes the identification between them and serves to reinforce the importance of Alan's first ride at the age of six and the role that horses play in his adolescent life. Finally, there is Hesther Salomon, the magistrate who leads Alan to Dr. Dysart. She is a sounding board for Dysart as well as a shoulder for him to cry on. She accepts none of his arguments about his disservice to Alan by making him normal. From her point of view, Alan is in pain, and Dysart's obligation is to relieve that pain. In her name, Shaffer has revealed her essence. Her given name is a form of Esther, the beautiful and compassionate biblical queen whose sense of justice saved her people from destruction. Her last name symbolizes the wisdom of her biblical namesake. Dysart's name is not without its symbolic value. The Greek prefix *dys* indicates difficulty,[5] and therefore shows that although he is performing his art (the second syllable of his name) masterfully, he does it in spite of himself. Ironically, the name of one of the therapists who is Dysart's colleague is Dr. Thoroughgood, in whose abilities Mrs. Salomon has no faith.

III *Sources, Symbols, and Themes*

Shaffer did extensive research before writing *Equus*, and the play is therefore enhanced by psychological, biblical, mythological, historical, and literary references. The time-honored symbols are horses, eyes, and tunnels. The compelling story aside, *Equus* is constructed on the basis of modern psychiatry, about which Shaffer consulted a child psychiatrist. The basic psychological issue in the play is presented in the writing of Dr. R. D. Laing, who questions the value and justice of curing many of those individuals whom society considers insane. He believes that man is born into a world where alienation awaits him (as with Alan), and that the diseases that psychiatrists purport to cure are really perpetuated when an individual is regarded as "object-to-be-changed" rather than "person-to-be-accepted." He further believes that more attention should be paid to the experience of the patient and that it should not be considered *ipso facto* invalid or unreal. Laing also objects to the denigration that the patient suffers when he is subjected to the process of psychiatric examination, diagnosis, and treatment.[6] Similarly, Anthony Burgess, in his popular novel and film, *A Clockwork Orange,* questions the right of society to cure a patient by removing from his personality the antisocial traits that make him unique. Martin Dysart exemplifies C. G. Jung's theory, too, that the more complicated and sophisticated he becomes, the more man loses the ability to follow his instincts.

The central symbol of the horse figures prominently in literary sources from the Bible to Homer, from Lawrence to Lorca, as well as in sources both mythological and historical. Biblical references to horses in *Equus* come from the Book of Job and from Revelation. The quotation in Job 39:19 - 25 refers to the horse's strength, speed, and fierceness:

Hast thou given the horse *his* might? Hast thou clothed his neck with the quivering mane? Hast thou made him to leap as a locust? The glory of his snorting is terrible. He paweth in the valley, and rejoiceth in his strength: He goeth out to meet the armed men. He mocketh at fear, and is not dismayed; Neither turneth he back from the sword. The quiver rattleth against him, The flashing spear and the javelin. He swallowth the ground with fierceness and rage; Neither believeth he that it is the voice of the trumpet. As oft as the trumpet *soundeth* he saith, Aha! And he smelleth the battle afar off, The thunder of the captains, and the shouting.[7]

The words of which this selection is composed are prominent in Alan's orgasmic rides: the *might,* the *neck,* the *mane,* the *trumpet,* and the *Aha!* And at the end of Alan's ride in Act One, the stage directions specify that the horse snorts, as in the previous selection. Similarly, the equine references in Revelation figure prominently in the play and in Alan's ideas of horses. Revelation 9:19 speaks of the "power of the horses [that] is in their mouth"; 6:2 - 8 attribute to horses the power of speech and the authority to kill with the sword; from Revelations 19:11 - 12 come the references to horses' eyes and the words that Alan uses in the blinding scene: "And I saw the heaven opened; and behold, a white horse, and he that sat thereon called Faithful and True. . . . And his eyes *are* a flame of fire . . . and he hath a name written which none knoweth but he himself." The first time Dysart asks Alan for the name of his horse-god, the boy refuses to answer because "no one knows but him and me" (p. 65). In 19:16, the identification between the horse and Jesus is established: "And he hath on his garment and on his thigh a name written, KING OF KINGS, AND LORD OF LORDS." Lastly, in the first chapter, verse fourteen, of Revelation, Jesus is described: "And his head and his hair were white wool, *white* as snow; and his eyes were as a flame of fire. . . ."

It is significant that Dysart's interest be for the classical world, since horses held an honored place in the ancient Greek society, even to the point of being considered beings of godly origin from the union of Poseidon and Demeter.[8] Significantly, too, the first horse that Alan ever rode was called Trojan, recalling the wooden horse in Book Eight of the *Odyssey*. Simpson[9] says that the Greeks raised aesthetic appreciation of horses to a pitch that has never been surpassed. The classicist Julian Ward Jones, Jr., in his article "The Trojan Horse, *Timeo Danaos et dona ferentis*," underscores the religious value of horses to the Trojans: "We can in no way consider it strange if to the Trojans—horse tamers extraordinary—the horse should sooner or later be regarded as a sacred animal. I suggest that this is exactly what happened and that the wooden horse was a religious object."[10] Lewinsohn, again in *Animals, Men and Myths*, sums up the role of horses in Homeric poetry and after: "In Homer's verse and thereafter the horse was an adjunct of the great heroes of ancient Greece, the greatest warriors rode on wonder beasts given to them by the gods. Most of these horses had wings, and many were able to talk" (p. 85). Like Xanthos in Book Nineteen of the *Iliad*, Equus is a "talking" horse. Many of the other horses in epic literature were named and prominent in legend: Alexander's Bucephalus, Roland's Veillantif, and the Cid's Babieca. In *Don Quixote*, the ingenious *hidalgo* spends four days deciding upon a name for his horse before settling on Rocinante. In ancient art, horses abound on Greek pottery and appear in the caves of Altamira, whose paintings are considered the oldest in the world. The cave-dwellers of what is now northern Spain depicted on their walls the animals that they feared and revered.

D. H. Lawrence is the link between ancient Greek mythology and modern British literature. In his *Etruscan Places* there are numerous references to horses in classical civilization. In the essay on "The Painted Tombs of Tarquinia" there is the reference to the young noblemen, who, according to Lawrence, surely rode with their own naked limbs against an almost naked horse. For Alan, nakedness is a *sine qua non* for riding Equus, and horses for him are: ". . . the most naked thing you ever saw! More than a dog or a cat or anything" (p. 48). Christopher Ford quotes Shaffer on the Homeric importance of the nakedness: "There's something Homeric about these encounters. I'm sure Ulysses was really naked when he chopped up all of those suitors."[11] Lawrence describes riding a horse as: ". . . A surge of animal power that burned with travel, with the passionate movement of the blood . . ."[12]—the same power and passion that Alan experiences when he mounts Equus. Lawrence asks rhetorically, "What is it that man sees, when he looks at a horse?—what is it that will never be put into words?" (p. 72). In "Volterra" he answers his own question: "The horse is always the symbol of the strong animal of man; sometimes he rises, a sea-horse, from the ocean: and sometimes he is a land creature, and half-man. And so he occurs on the tombs, as the passion in man returning into the sea, the soul retreating into the death-world at the depths of the waters: or sometimes he is a centaur . . ." (p. 108). In a short story, "The Rocking-Horse Winner," the horse becomes Lawrence's central image, in a way that closely parallels Shaffer's use of it in *Equus*. In the Lawrence story, Paul, the young protagonist, "hears" the voice of the rocking-horse predicting winners in horse races; and the gardener becomes terribly serious when he is discussing horses, ". . . as if he were speaking of religious matters. . . ."[13] Lawrence makes repeated references to the fire in Paul's eyes; and most important, the boy rides his rocking horse with the orgasmic furor with which Alan rides Equus.

García Lorca used horses as a major symbol in both his plays and his poems.[14] In "Quimera" (Chimera), a one-act play, Viejo (Old Man) speaks of his fear of horses: "Los caballos, ¡jajaja! Nadie sabe el miedo que a mí me dan los caballos. Caiga un rayo sobre todos sus ojos."[15] (Horses, ha-ha-ha! Nobody knows how afraid I am of horses. I wish lightning would strike out their eyes.)[16] He later makes another statement which equates sexual satisfaction and fecundity with love of horses, and hippophobia with sexual unfulfillment. In *La zapatera prodigiosa* (previously mentioned), *La casa de Bernarda Alba* (The House of Bernarda Alba), and *Bodas de sangre* (Blood Wedding), horses appear as symbols of manhood, force, and sexual desire. At the time of Lorca's murder, the playwright had not yet completed all of the plays that he wanted to write—a body of works that was to examine love in all of its many facets. One of the plays which was never written was going to be about a boy who is so devoted to his horse that, when the boy's father kills the horse, the boy, in turn, kills his father. The fact that the story of *Equus* is based on an actual happening in no way diminishes the importance of the equine imagery. The account that Shaffer heard of the event was merely the spark that ignited his imagination and creative powers on the archetypal symbol.

Eyes, too, are rich in symbolic value and have held a place in literature at least since St. Matthew wrote: "And if thy right eye causeth you to stumble, pluck it out, and cast it from thee . . ." (5:29). Latin uses the same word *testis* for both *witness* and *testicle*, thereby showing the relationship between eyes, which are literal witnesses, and testicles, which are figurative witnesses.[17] In the first scene of the play in which Alan is willing to talk to Dysart without resorting to television jingles, he displays his knowledge of English history, knowledge that he acquired from his mother and of which he is very proud. His favorite king, he tells the doctor, is John: "Because he put out the eyes of that smarty little—" (p. 28). This reference helps to unravel the connection of imagery as it exists in Alan's mind. It is known, for example, that of the men whom John took prisoner, some were blinded; and that when Arthur became a rival of John, John was advised to have Arthur blinded and castrated.[18] The instance which most closely approximates the situation in *Equus* occurs in a one-act play entitled "Los ojos" (The Eyes), by José Ruibal. In this play, a child who can no longer stand his mother's nagging and her insistence that her eyes see everything—including through walls and into dreams—takes a knife, stabs out her eyes, and ends the play by telling her, "Tus ojos ya no lo verán todo . . . , todo . . . , todo . . ." (p. 63).[19] (Now your eyes won't see everything . . . , everything . . . , everything. . . .)

Animals' eyes appear in the writing of many authors. In any number of works by García Lorca, for example, he refers to eyes, and in one poem, "Oda al rey de Harlem" (Ode to the King of Harlem), in his collection *El poeta en Nueva York* (The Poet in New York), he uses crocodiles to symbolize unadulterated, primitive society, and a spoon to represent destructive civilization; the spoon is used to gouge out the eyes of the crocodiles:

> Con una cuchara,
> arrancaba los ojos a los cocodrilos

y golpeaba el trasero de los monos.
Con una cuchara. (p. 478)

(With a spoon, he pulled out the crocodiles' eyes and beat the
monkeys' behinds. With a spoon.) A recent example is the short
story "Axolotl" (Salamander), by the Argentine writer Julio Cor-
tázar—a story in which the protagonist is metamorphosed into a
lizard by staring into its eyes. Through his deep attraction for the
animals, he becomes one of them, just as Alan attempts to become
One Person with Equus. An old superstition holds that boys who
masturbate excessively will go blind. Ironically, in the play it is the
masturbator who blinds the object of his lust. Christopher Ford
mentioned that Shaffer would like to write a play on the Faust
theme.[20] For Shaffer, the blinded Faust got something positive and
even ecstatic from his transformation to blindness.

One final symbol is that of the tunnel. The set calls for two
onstage sections of seats, which are separated by a central tunnel. It
is through this tunnel that horse/horseman Nugget enters into and
exits from Alan's life. Tunnels are womblike, and this one may be
interpreted as the place where Alan receives his sexual gratification.
It may also be thought of as the dark recesses of the psyche, which
Lawrence considered the places where the soul of the horse prances.
For Alan, horses are like graceful girls in a ballet.

IV   *Structure and Stagecraft*

The two acts of which *Equus* is composed are parallel in their
structure. Each act begins with a monologue in which Dysart
wonders about the horse, the boy, and himself. Many of the scenes
take place between two characters having a go at each other, as in a
boxing ring. The last scene of each act has a highly dramatic moment with sexual and religious overtones, acted out by Alan. The
first act ends with the young man riding Equus to orgasm and with
words from the Old Testament; the second act contains an equally
dramatic nude scene of attempted intercourse, the blinding of the
horses, and words from the New Testament.

The temporal and the spatial organization of the play merit
special attention. Dysart's opening monologue in each act takes
place in the present, as do some of the therapy sessions with Alan.
The scenes in which Dysart is narrating events that happened in
sessions that took place between scenes and the incidents that in-

volve Alan's childhood and the night of his crime are flashbacks. Most of the play takes place in the doctor's consultation room, with departures for scenes in the Strangs' home, the movie theater, the electrical shop, and, of course, the stables. In scenes in which Alan is not present in the office but rather in his hospital room, he is able to hear the conversation taking place and to comment on it as if he were together with the other characters. For example, when Dora is telling Dysart of the passage about horses in the Book of Job, she recites one line, and Alan responds with the next. When Frank is telling the psychiatrist about the scene in the bedroom, where Alan was beating himself and reciting a parody of biblical genealogies, Alan speaks the words that he was reciting that night.

The text of the play is preceded by notes on the set, the chorus, and the horses. The set is described as a square of wood set in a circle of wood, with rails on three sides contaiining benches. The stage has the aspect of an operating theater from which the part of the audience seated onstage witnesses at close range Dysart's metaphorical operation on Alan's mind. Also, the theater has the appearance of one appropriate for the performance of Greek tragedy. Shaffer has the seated members of the cast—that is, the chorus—making "Equus Noise" of humming, thumping, and stamping. "This Noise heralds or illustrates the presence of Equus the God" (p. 13). The horses are actors wearing chestnut-colored tracksuits, high metal shoes, and masks made of alternating bands of wire and leather. The playwright specifies that "any literalism which could suggest the cosy familiarity of a domestic animal—or worse, a pantomime horse—should be avoided. . . . Great care must also be taken that the masks are put on before the audience with very precise timing—the actors watching each other, so that the masking has an exact and ceremonial effect" (p. 13). Shaffer's intent is that the horses have an archetypal character about them, appearing as ceremonial gods, as it is most evident in the stage directions of the blinding scene:

He stabs out Nugget's eyes. The horse stamps in agony. A great screaming begins to fill the theatre. growing ever louder. Alan dashes at the other two horses and blinds them too, stabbing over the rails. Their metal hooves join in the stamping.
Relentlessly, as this happens, three more horses appear in cones of light: not naturalistic animals like the first three, but dreadful creatures out of nightmare. Their eyes flare—their nostrils flare—their mouths flare. They are archetypal images—judging, punishing, pitiless. They do not halt at the

*rail, but invade the square. As they trample at him, the boy leaps desperate-
ly at them, jumping high and naked in the dark, slashing at their heads
with arms upraised. (p. 103)*

Five Finger Exercise and *Shrivings* are true to the spirit of the
classical unities, but *Equus*, both in its dramatic theory and in its ex-
ecution, much more nearly approximates true Aristotelian tragedy.
Acording to Aristotle, "A tragedy, then, is the imitation of an action
that is serious and also, as having magnitude, complete in itself; in
language with pleasurable accessories, each kind brought in
separately in the parts of the work; in a dramatic, not in a narrative
form; with incidents arousing pity and fear, wherewith to ac-
complish its catharsis of such emotions."[21] He further said that
"tragedy is essentially an imitation not of persons but of action and
life, of happiness and misery . . ." (p. 231), preferably based on
historical events, and with personages of distinctive qualities of
character and thought, and consistent in their behavior throughout
the play. *Equus* fulfills all of the master's requirements for tragedy.
Aristotle recommended that the tragedian describe what *might*
have happened, not what did happen. *Equus* imitates an actual
event, modified to proportions suitable for the stage and interpreted
in the inimitable manner of Peter Shaffer. The characters contrast
the emotions of ecstasy and joylessness. The incidents in the play in-
spire pity for Dysart and both fear and pity for Alan. Shaffer also
satisfies the six qualitative parts of Aristotelian tragedy: plot,
character, diction, thought, spectacle, and melody. Aristotle's intention in the category of "thought" was that the play enunciate a
general truth. The truth that Shaffer presents is one that shocks the
audience, but also one that wins its approval.

Shaffer, like Aristotle, believes that the most important element
of a play is its story.[22] An essential element of the plot according to
Aristotle is that of discovery. *Equus* is based on the discoveries or insights that Dr. Dysart makes and has into Alan's problem, often via
information brought to him from characters who function as the
messengers in Greek tragedy: Frank Strang, Dora Strang, and
Harry Dalton. He also makes perceptive discoveries about himself.
For the Greek theoretician, melody was the greatest of the
pleasurable accessories of tragedy, and in *Equus* it is found in Alan's
wild song to Equus the lover and Equus the god during his frantic
ride. Spectacle is found in every aspect of the play, from the onstage
seating to the stylized horse masks. Perhaps Shaffer's greatest
success in *Equus* is in fulfilling the requirements that the story of

the play represent ". . . one action, a complete whole, with its several incidents so closely connected that the transposal or withdrawal of any one of them will disjoin and dislocate the whole" (p. 234). Shaffer's crafting is meticulous; ingeniously he presents the details of Alan's case bit by bit and has Dysart reach his conclusions by connecting each piece of new information to that which he already knows. If any of the information were omitted, there would be no play, or at least not in the stage of perfection to which Shaffer has designed it. Aristotle preferred that the plot be episodic, with neither probability nor necessity in the sequence of its episodes. To that end, Shaffer moves back and forth in time in Dysart's search for the root of Alan's motivations. Shaffer, as Aristotle, specifies that the action of the play is continuous.

Both writers knew that the events which arouse fear and pity are most effective when they occur unexpectedly yet at the same time in consequence of one another. In the case of *Equus,* those events are Alan's midnight ride and his blinding of the horses, an act which also displays the Aristotelian property of suffering or torture. The final monologue, which follows Alan's reenactment of his crime, is equivalent to the catharsis in Greek tragedy. As its quantitative parts, Aristotle specifies prologue, episode, exode, and chorus. Dysart's opening monologue is the prologue; his closing speech is the exode; the therapy sessions are the episodes; and the actors onstage making the "Equus Noise" are the chorus. An equally important aspect of classical tragedy that Shaffer observes is that of the change from ignorance to knowledge. By examining the events that led up to Alan's crime, Dysart comes to understand not only his patient but also himself, and it is he who is the truly tragic hero, whose flaw, over which he has no control, is his joylessness, his emotional sterility.

V   *Critical Appraisal*

No other of Shaffer's plays has received so much attention from the critics as has *Equus.* From one extreme, it has been interpreted as a play about man's starvation for transcendence, a play which urges the spectator to examine the mysteries of the Christian faith.[23] At the other extreme, critics have seen in it a homosexual attraction between doctor and patient.[24] One critic went so far as to say that the play is an attempt on the part of the author to present a defense of homosexuality, and a dishonest one at that.[25] Most criticism falls short of those extreme positions and views the play as a confrontation between reason and instinct, in a well-constructed, psychological mystery play. Reviewers generally showed a keen understanding and appreciation of the play and did not spare superlatives in their reviews. *Equus* has been called an electrifying theatrical experience[26] and a theatrical event of the greatest importance;[27] it has been hailed as one of the most powerful and provocative theatrical events of our time.[28] And so it is. The *New York Times*[29] raved about the play's stagecraft and sensibility and praised the work for reanimating the spirit of mystery that makes the theater a place of breathless discovery. The *New York Daily News*[30] thought that the psychoanalysis left something to be desired, but that the play made for gripping theater and powerful entertainment—results which, after all, fulfill Shaffer's intentions in writing it. Some reviewers voiced the same criticism of *Equus* that had previously appeared about *The Royal Hunt of the Sun:* the staging compensates for the faults of the script.[31] The *New Yorker* viewed the play as a "continuously exciting dance of exploration through the mind of a boy who loves horses, worships the quality of 'horseness,' and commits a dreadful crime in the name of that worship."[32] The last statement is at once the most precise and concise evaluation of the play's meaning and spirit. *Equus* is a masterfully crafted play, and if it is to be criticized at all, it is for being *too* perfect, too pat. The playwright has so carefully constructed it that there are no loose ends left for the audience to tie together; and yet the play has inspired such diverse interpretations.

Equus has received considerable attention from the psychiatric community. Dr. Jules Glenn, a psychiatrist in Great Neck, New York, has written considerably on Shaffer's plays;[33] at a meeting of the Association for Applied Psychoanalysis, there was a discussion of this play. But psychiatrists have not unanimously acclaimed it. In an article in the *New York Times*, Dr. Sanford Gifford, a professor at the medical school of Harvard University, objected that the analysis that Dr. Dysart uses on Alan is medically unsound and that the play fosters the fantasies that patients have of their therapists.[34] Whatever the medical men may decide, taking the play so seriously is a credit to Shaffer's talents and discussing Alan Strang as a patient elevates him to that level reserved for such towering figures of world literature as Don Quixote, Don Juan, Hamlet, and Lady Macbeth.

The success of *Equus* has been overwhelming in part because of its visual spectacle and its thought-provoking theme. But the reason for its widespread appeal is deeper than that; *Equus* touches the spectator at his most basic level of emotions. However sophisticated, the audience applauds the speech in which Dysart finds it ironic—ridiculous—that he, a passionless man, should be curing Alan, who knows ecstasy; however conventional their beliefs, the spectators deeply desire to be Alan—that is, to allow themselves to live on an instinctual and primitive level, free from societal restrictions, if only for an hour every three weeks. The appeal is so deep that one does not respond with polite applause, but with glee. Shaffer completely wins the audience over to Dysart's point of view that he is doing Alan a disservice by curing him. *Equus* compels each spectator to reevaluate "the old language and old assumptions" that he may have accepted uncritically and never before questioned. *Equus* is a guilt-relieving play; the average theatergoer comes to realize that whatever his little fantasies may be, they are trivial next to Alan's. Perhaps the imagery is, by intention, transparent; but *Equus* has given the theatergoer something for which he had been starved: compelling drama that keeps him on the edge of his seat and his eyes riveted to the stage.

For writing the best play of the 1974 - 75 New York theater season, Shaffer won the New York Drama Critics' Circle Award, the Antoinette Perry ("Tony") Award, as well as the Outer Critics Circle Award and the Los Angeles Drama Critics Award. *Equus*, more than anything else that he has written, has earned Peter Shaffer a permanent place in the history of British drama.

The relationship of *Equus* to Shaffer's other plays is appropriate material for this book's conclusion.

CHAPTER 7

Conclusion

T HE preface to this study focuses on the diversity of
Shaffer's plays; the conclusion, then, should emphasize the
unity of his work, from the early detective novels through *Equus*,
the play that is the culmination of all of the characters, themes, and
techniques that came before it. *Equus* has as its most dramatic
figure a deeply disturbed young man, who far surpasses in his
maladjustment any other character of Shaffer's creation. Alan's
forerunners (in a minor key) are Clive *(Five Finger Exercise)*, Bob
(The Private Ear), and David *(Shrivings)*. Clive has only begun to
explore his own nature. He is sorting through his confusion on who
he is and what he wants his life to be, but his behavior is never antisocial. Bob is a loner who spends his evenings "conducting" records
in his flat, but after his failure with Doreen all that he destroys is a
phonograph record. David's decision to leave Cambridge University
when failure is imminent hurts only himself and disappoints his
father. Alan's behavior is psychotic.

Alan's parents, too, may be traced through Shaffer's works. The
earliest, yet most closely related, situation exists in *The Woman in
the Wardrobe*, in which Mr. Verity reveals that his mother (married
to a man whom he considered "nothing" and someone that he
hardly knew) fell in love with a carpenter, an amorous attraction
which the neighbors considered the result of religious mania—an
early forerunner of Alan's religious mother and emotionally
alienated father. Alan's parents have precedents throughout
Shaffer's plays. The first disappointed father (also a successful
businessman) is Mr. Mayer in "The Salt Land." In truth, he is a
man twice disappointed: in Jo, who never shared his love for the
Torah, and in Arieh, who turns away from the Commandments and
ultimately kills his brother. In "The Prodigal Father," the son is
betrayed by his father, who estranged himself for sixteen years. The
father, though, is displeased that his son does not share what the

father considers his good taste. In *Five Finger Exercise* and *Shrivings,* the lack of understanding between the fathers and sons is also mutual. (In addition to Clive and his father, there is also Walter, whose father absented himself from his family for six years). Neither Stanley Harrington nor Frank Strang will ever see his son follow his father's tradition in business. The mothers are usually pretentious, socially conscious women. Alan's mother brags that her family was a member of the "horsey" set, just as Clive's mother allows no one to forget her French ancestry. Tom's mother *(The White Liars)* creates for her son an image acceptable for presentation to her bridge club. Sophie Weinberg (not a mother) has her whole life dominated by her social preoccupations, and Carol Melkett *(Black Comedy)* demonstrates through her materialistic attitude that she is following in the other women's footsteps.

The relationship between Alan's parents is considerably better than that of the Harringtons, the Sidleys *(The Public Eye),* or the Mayers (Arieh and Kulli), but still there are the strong differences over religion and social standing: like Louise Harrington, Dora Strang thinks that she married beneath herself. Alan's father believes that he lost his son to his wife, and thus echoes Stanley Harrington's major complaint against his wife. Although they were not physically estranged from their fathers as were Jed and David, Alan's and Clive's estrangement is an emotional one, and as a result the mother-figures are far more important than the father-figures in their lives. (In *Five Finger Exercise,* there are references to *Oedipus Rex* and *Electra,* both of which are prototypes of an unnatural attraction of a child for a parent.) Ted undermines Bob's masculinity in *The Private Ear* by telling Doreen what a good son Bob is to his mother. There is no mention of a father. Lois Neal is no one's mother, but she makes the rules and the decisions for David and for Gideon at Shrivings. The possessiveness of one person over another extends beyond the realm of a mother for her son (strongly in *Five Finger Exercise,* less so in *Equus*) and into other relationships as well: Lady Sylvia over Lucy ("The Prodigal Father"), Frank over Tom *(The White Liars),* and Miss Whitely over Hilary Stanton *(Withered Murder).*

For want of any real relationship with his father, Alan tries to adopt Dr. Dysart as much as the doctor tries to adopt Alan as his son. Their relationship resembles those of Young Martin with Pizarro and David with Gideon. In a similar vein, Pizarro and Atahuallpa adopt each other as brothers in an alliance as deadly as that of Arieh with his real brother, Jo.

The passionless marriage of the Dysarts recalls those of the Harringtons (who barely tolerate each other), the Askelons (Mark grew to hate his wife), and the Petries (whose relationship was sexless and not much more stimulating that Enid's second marriage, which consists of two partners skimming Ovaltine for each other). Private fantasy sometimes replaces marriage's intimacy. Dysart's fantasy is one which he is free to indulge at home: reading books about the Greek civilization. Charles Sidley and Frank Strang have to be more covert about their private lives; for one reason or another, both of them have to go outside of their marriages for sexual fulfillment: Sidley to a Notting Hill Gate prostitute, and Strang alone to an adult cinema.

The least developed character of any consequence in *Equus* is Jill Mason, whose function is to lead Alan to a job with horses, to the pornographic theater where he discovers his father, and to the stables where Alan discovers his impotence. Her character derives from Lucy's in "The Prodigal Father," who is undeveloped and remains unchanged in the course of the script and merely an antagonist against whom to develop the personalities of Lady Sylvia, Jed, and Leander. Of all of the characters in the Harrington household, the perceptive Pamela is the least individualized. Similarly, Carol Melkett is one-dimensional (which is reasonable in a comedy of stock characters), but Brindsley is not; he is given depth, and his actions, motivation. Doreen, in *The Private Ear*, is never given enough attention for the reader to know her as an individual rather than a type. Lois Neal in *Shrivings* suffers as much of a loss as any of the men in the play, but does not succeed in winning the reader's sympathy.

Shaffer's characters demonstrate a wide range of sexual preferences. In *Withered Murder*, an attraction between two women is considered the motivation for the murder. Tom (*The White Liars*) makes it clear that the attention that Frank pays to Sue is just so much posturing and that his real attraction is to Tom. Harold Gorringe, the flamboyant homosexual of *Black Comedy*, is a comical figure, but one whose feelings are real to him. Just as Louise makes insinuations about Clive's attraction for Walter, Mark accuses Gideon of having a sexual appetite only for slim, brown boys; Gideon claims that as a youth he reacted with equal sexual stimulation to males, females, dogs, flowers, political science, and mathematics. Clive is preoccupied with his sexuality; Bob's is still unknown to him; David's attraction is equally divided between Lois and Gideon; and Alan can find sexual satisfaction only during his wild rides on Equus.

Sexually, some of the men fancy themselves Don Juans; others, failures; some, both. Ted and Brindsley are the most obvious Don Juans. Mark Askelon and Frank (*The White Liars*) would like to have the world believe that they are sexual champions with women, which is untrue in both cases. Jed, Bob, Julian (*The Public Eye*), Pizarro, and Dysart are realistic with themselves about the importance of women in their lives and of their appeal to the opposite sex. Tom in *White Lies* and Frank in *The White Liars* wish that they could be more attractive to the women that they love. For Clive, the question of women remains remote from his life. Alan's sexuality is the cause of his criminal act: he attempts to replace Equus with Jill as the source of his sexual gratification and discovers that his jealous god will keep him forever impotent with women.

Many of the characters live with their sights set on the future and with their trust placed in others; their hopes and trusts are short-lived. Arieh's hope for the future is in a homeland in which the Jewish people may be free. However, he murders his brother, and his own future is in a prison cell. Like Moses, he led his people, but never enjoyed the milk and honey of the Promised Land. Walter and Clive both have visions of their futures, which, because of their mutual trust, they share with each other. Their trust and their hopes shatter, and they are resigned to living one day at a time. Bob had hoped that he could establish at least a friendship with a woman, and to that end he trusted in the help of his friend Ted. His hope, his trust, and his friend are all lost to him after his evening with Doreen. Pizarro is trusted by both Young Martin and Atahuallpa, both of whom he betrays.[1] *He* trusted in Atahuallpa's godly powers to transcend death, but that, too, never came to pass. In a comic situation Harold Gorringe, who makes much of how he always trusted Brindsley, ultimately suffers disappointment (which he greatly exaggerates) and discards his former friend. The ultimate trust is Alan's for Dr. Dysart. He entrusts him with his most intimate and embarrassing secrets and bares himself completely before the doctor in hopes of being freed from the torment of his crime. Dysart believes, however, that Alan would be better to run away and to keep his passion intact rather than to allow the psychiatrist to cure him of it.

The result of misplaced hopes and trust is often an alienated soul groping through life. Such is the situation of Walter and of the Harringtons at the end of *Five Finger Exercise*, of Bob at the end of *The Private Ear*, of Frank at the end of *The White Liars*, of Martin in *The Royal Hunt of the Sun*, and of all who spent the weekend at Shrivings. There is a feeling of temporary reconciliation of differences of the Harringtons, between Mark and David, between Jed and Leander, and probably a lasting change for Lucy and Lady Sylvia. Perhaps even Alan will be reconciled with society, if not with his parents.

The sources of worship vary from play to play and from character to character. For Arieh, the source is the Torah, the 5,000-year-old heritage of his people. Bob adores music. Pizarro wishes that he could share the Incas' worship of the sun. Frank thinks of Tom as a monster who thrives on receiving worship. Many of the characters revere each other: Frank, Tom; David and Lois, Gideon; Mark and Giulia, each other. Alan worships Equus. The characters whose inspiration is in religion (Arieh and Dora) are far outnumbered by the skeptics, the agnostics, and the atheists: Jo, Pizarro, Lois, Mark, and Frank Strang. Contempt for religion, churches, and their officers appears first in *The Woman in the Wardrobe* and reaches its most distressing depths in *The Royal Hunt of the Sun*, *Shrivings*, and *Equus*, with ridicule expressed by Pizarro, Mark, and Frank. Spain's priests are presented as inhumane; Mark views nuns as sadists, whipping children into belief; Mr. Strang holds religion responsible for his son's masochism and for the horrible crime. The metaphorical cannibalism of which Clive warns Walter is misconstrued as physical practice when Atahuallpa misunderstands the Spaniards' explanation of Communion. Mark ridicules the passion for invisible gods, and Dysart regrets that he must exorcise from Alan the worship of his horse-god and replace it with a belief in the "abstract" God. Religion for Shaffer's characters is the source of the Voice. It calls to Arieh to use the sword for the good of his people. Alan "hears" Equus's disapproval and is impotent with Jill. [2]

With anticipatory, unconscious irony, Mr. Fathom in *Withered Murder* cautions meditation before falling victim to the follies of youthful passion. But some characters, like Gideon and Alan, live for their passions and, in turn, are nurtured by them. The pathetic characters are the ones who cannot feel passion: Pizarro, Mark, and Dysart. These men are resigned to an emptiness in their lives and can never know the satisfaction that Gideon derives from his philosophy, that Atahuallpa derives from the sun, that Julian

derives from his deep knowledge of and belief in himself, or that
Alan used to derive from horses.

From his earliest novels, Shaffer's works have been based on peo-
ple in competition with each other, from the adulterous activities in
How Doth the Little Crocodile? and the lesbian overtones in
Withered Murder to the triangles (and rectangles) which exist in the
plays: Clive vs. Walter and Stanley for Louise's attention; Ted vs.
Bob for Doreen's; Tom vs. Frank for Sue's love; Mark vs. Gideon
for David's affection. There is Jed against Lady Sylvia for Lucy;
Clea against Carol for Brindsley; and Jill against Equus for Alan.

The techniques that prevail are games, tricks, and lies. Clive
plays a *poseur* game to keep the favor of his mother, while Walter
wears an orphan's mask to hide his true identity from the world.
Louise's game is nicknames, in which Walter is Hibou, the Owl, the
same name that Gideon uses for David. Ted wears a mask of
friendship before Bob, but secretly connives to win Doreen away
from him. *White Lies* and *The White Liars* are nonstop rounds of
image-games on the part of the rock singers and the managers,
Sophie, and the singers' mothers (who never appear onstage).
Ironically enough, Mr. Fathom warned about the ends of self-
deception in *Withered Murder*. The idle threat of telling Belinda
that her husband pays regular visits to a prostitute persuades
Charles to play along with Julian's prescribed silence game and to
allow the former detective to play at being an accountant. The light
game in *Black Comedy* is the device that allows Brindsley to shed
his metaphorical mask that he never before had the self-confidence
to discard. (The masks are physical in *The Royal Hunt of the Sun*,
Equus, and *The Woman in the Wardrobe*.) Mark challenges
Shrivings to play an apple game with him, and four lives are forever
changed. There is game-playing in full bloom in *Equus*, in which
the games become increasingly sophisticated in order to get Alan to
reveal himself to his psychiatrist.

Another motif that appears in Shaffer's three major plays is that
of dreams. It is the clue to the playwright's method in *Five Finger
Exercise;* to Pizarro's preoccupation with Atahuallpa, of whom he
dreamed every night until finally they met; and to the strong effect
that Alan has on Dr. Dysart—strong enough to produce nightmares
almost as distressing as Alan's.

An element common to all of Shaffer's plays and novels are the
references to the classical world and/or modern Greece. The novels
are permeated with the art and archaeology of the ancients. *Five*

Finger Exercise and *The White Liars* refer to *Oedipus Rex* and *Electra;* the picture in Bob's room is of Venus; Julian boasts that his father is a Rhodes scholar (that is, a scholar from Rhodes). Sophie's former boyfriends are from Greece, and Mark resides in Corfu. Dr. Dysart wishes that he lived somewhere along the Greek coast, where the gods used to bathe.

There are messages in the plays, sometimes made evident in monologues, at other times through the dialogue. Dysart exposes the play's message in his didactic speeches to Hesther and to the audience. Clive attempts to instruct his father in the reasons for education. De Nizza blasts the Inca system, which precludes suffering and deprivation. Pizarro, Lois, and Mark all make speeches that are antireligion, antipatriotism, essentially antiestablishment. The idea of the destructiveness of conventionality (or at least its lack of creativity) concerns the characters in "The Salt Land," in which Arieh is disgusted by his brother's normality, as well as in *Five Finger Exercise, The Public Eye,* and *Equus,* where traditional views are considered unfulfilling by Clive, Julian, Belinda, and Dysart. Nontraditional acts are defended in a work as early as *Withered Murder,* in which Mr. Fathom, the genius of the novel, defends some healthy sadism in a marriage. (From the other extreme, passivism is the issue in "The Salt Land" and in *Shrivings.*) There is a preoccupation with the search for a promised land and for immortality. Arieh and Pizarro look to Israel and Peru as the end of the rainbow. They also long to have their names sung in ballads. Mark's bid for immortality is through his poetry. Mr. Fathom talks of his attempts to discover immortality and compares them to those of Ptolemy II; immortality, he believes, comes by living every day of one's life.

Lack of place, homelessness, is a theme that finds its way into the plays from "The Salt Land," in which the Jews are wandering from Europe to Israel, to *Shrivings,* in which Mark bemoans the fact that his son will always be a "mongrel" and never know a place that he can call his home; from *Five Finger Exercise,* in which Walter has left his homeland behind, to Dysart's last monologue in *Equus,* in which he fears that industrialized, modern life, symbolized by multi-lane highways, may one day extinguish altogether the very idea of Place.

Hands and eyes are the two parts of the body that are constants in Shaffer's work. Bob gives a poetic and moving description of the creation and abuse of hands, and Louise regrets that Clive does not play the piano even though he has the hands with which to be good at it. In "The Salt Land" and *Equus,* hands are the tools of destruction to strangle Jo and to stab out the horses' eyes. Eyes have a long tradition in Shaffer's work also. They are described by Bob in the same speech in which he talks about hands; and in the companion play, Julian describes in detail his Public Eyes. Eyes are one of the sources of Sophie's attraction for Vassili and for her making an association between him and Tom in *White Lies.* Likewise, Pizarro notices Atahuallpa's coal black eyes. Eyes are a physical sign of beauty (Lois's and Giulia's), or a disgusting part of the body (Gideon's). In *Equus,* Jill says that for her they are the sexiest part of a man's body, and Alan has a fascination for horses' eyes that makes him stare at them endlessly. Finally, they are the object of his vengeance against Equus.

Sharp objects as tools of destruction appear and reappear. Arieh uses a knife rather than a gun in the war for a free State of Israel. Bob uses a phonograph needle to scratch a recording of *Madame Butterfly* beyond repair. Colonel Melkett and Harold Gorringe take pointed objects from a piece of Brindsley's sculpture and chase him around the room with them. (Sidley threatens Julian with a ruler, which does not strictly qualify as a sharp object, and Mark warns—and proves—that the tongue can be the sharpest weapon of all.) The most devastating use of a sharp object is Alan's blinding of six horses with a metal pick.

Horses figure in two plays before *Equus. The Royal Hunt of the Sun* has an implied reference to horses; horse and rider were considered godly beings. (Historically, Atahuallpa enjoyed watching De Soto's skills in horsemanship.)[3] And in *Five Finger Exercise* Pamela is dressed in jodhpurs for riding, and she has a friend who lives over the stables.

A variety of minor elements give unity to Shaffer's work. There are a preponderance of Germans, for example. One of the suspects in *Withered Murder* is a professor from Germany. Walter, Sophie, and Schuppanzigh (the electrician in *Black Comedy*) are all German, and all three share the traits of hidden or mistaken identities. Germans lurk in the background as the Jews flee from Europe in "The Salt Land," and in Mark's reference to Nazis. The Bible suggested the title of "The Salt Land" and "The Prodigal Father." Gideon's name appears twice, once in a quotation in "The Salt Land" and later as one of the protagonists of *Shrivings.* In both works, there is a chair of glory: the one that makes Mark jealous of

Gideon, and Arieh's chair at the command post, to which Jo refers sarcastically as "the seat of glory." Cambridge is the university of Clive Harrington and Mark Askelon, and almost of David, too. Bob calls his stereo set Behemoth, the name used for a beast in the Book of Job. Music is an important element. It is the heart and soul of Bob's life—all that he has to sustain him and to get him from one ordinary day to the next. *White Lies* and *The White Liars* use rock musicians as part of the casts. Atahuallpa demonstrates that he is aware of Pizarro's plans to rob the Incas of their gold in his song, "O Little Finch." A stuck needle on a record leads to the discovery of Walter's suicide attempt. His knowledge of music is one of Louise's reasons for feeling an attraction for Walter, and his lack of appreciation of it is a weapon that she uses against Stanley in her war of snobbery. The structure and title of *Five Finger Exercise* were both suggested by music for piano.

Each of Shaffer's plays unconsciously anticipates the next. The musical substructure of *Five Finger Exercise* becomes a dominant theme in *The Private Ear;* the Pygmalionlike relationship in *The Private Ear* forecasts the relationship between the Sidleys in *The Public Eye.*[4] Charles Sidley's attraction to the sun as a source of youth anticipates Pizarro's hunt for the sun; and the horse-gods of the Spanish *conquistadores* become for Alan the godslave, Equus.

Now that Shaffer is enjoying the height of his success, where does his career go from here? Responding to a question about his future plans, he replied, "God knows what my plans are for the future! Plays. I hope and pray."[5]

And so do we all.

Notes and References

Preface

1. Except in the chapter on *Shrivings*, where this organization is less appropriate than in the other chapters.

2. See, for example, Robert Brustein, *The Theatre of Revolt: An Approach to Modern Drama* (Boston, 1974); Ruby Cohn, *Currents in Contemporary Drama* (Bloomington, IN, 1969); John Elsom, *Post-War British Theatre* (London, 1976); Martin Esslin, *The Theater of the Absurd* (Garden City, NY, 1969); Arnold P. Hinchliffe, *British Theatre 1950 - 70* (Totowa, NJ, 1974); Frederick Lumley, *New Trends in Twentieth Century Drama: A Survey since Ibsen and Shaw* (New York, 1967); J. L. Styan, *The Dark Comedy: The Development of Modern Comic Tragedy* (Cambridge, England, 1962); John Russell Taylor, *The Angry Theatre: New British Drama* (New York, 1969); George Wellwarth, *The Theater of Protest and Paradox: Developments in the Avant-Garde Drama* (New York, 1964).

3. Such as Hinchliffe's study on *Harold Pinter*.

Chapter One

1. Shaffer's plays have been so successful all over the world that it would be meaningless to mention the number of performances of each work in London and New York.

2. Two of the sketches that Shaffer wrote for the British television series "That Was the Week That Was" appear in a collection by the same name. The intention of the program was as much to be topical and satirical as it was to be comical and entertaining. The first of Shaffer's two contributions is "But My Dear," a one-scene dialogue between Senior Officer and Junior Officer (whose name is Fairy) on "good taste" in letters. The conversation evolves into a comic and ironic tirade against homosexuals by Senior Officer. The second piece is called "The President of France" and is a satirical speech delivered by the chauvinistic French President in 1990 to the Council of Europe. Both pieces are as pointed and biting as they are creative and entertaining.

3. Peter Shaffer in "Labels Aren't for Playwrights," *Theatre Arts* (February 1960), p. 21.

4. Don Ross, "Peter Shaffer Is an Enemy of 'Togetherness,' " *New York Herald Tribune* (January 3, 1960), section four, p. 3.

5. The British "Pantomine" for children is a traditional Christmas time entertainment; it is not mime theater.

6. "Joan Littlewood Panto," December 20, 1963, p. 7.

7. December 20, 1963, p. 18.

8. December 20, 1963, p. 4.

9. December 20, 1963, p. 13.

10. December 20, 1963, p. 4.

11. December 22, 1963, p. 14.

Chapter Two

1. Peter Shaffer, *Five Finger Exercise* (London, 1958), p. 1.

2. "Labels," pp. 20 - 21.

3. Ross, p. 3.

4. ". . . One day he [Shaffer] picked up a book labeled 'Five Finger Exercises' . . . for the exercise of five interrelated elements and how they react to one another and how they strengthen each other, or weaken each other if you use them wrong." From Joseph A. Loftus, "Playwright's Moral Exercise," *New York Times,* November 29, 1959, section two, p. 3.

5. "Strangers at Breakfast," *Reporter* 22 (January 7, 1960), pp. 36 - 37.

6. *Anger and After: New British Drama* (New York, 1969), p. 275.

7. *McGraw Hill Encyclopedia of World Drama* (New York, 1972), volume 4, pp. 83 - 85.

8. Review in *Observer* (July 20, 1958), p. 13.

9. December 12, 1959, pp. 100 - 102.

10. Review in the *New York Journal American,* December 3, 1959; *NYTCR,* 1959, p. 207.

11. "Playwright's Moral Exercise," p. 1.

12. Review in the *New York Daily Mirror,* December 3, 1959; and *NYTCR,* 1959, p. 210.

13. *The Theater of Protest and Paradox: Developments in the Avant-Garde Drama* (New York, 1964), p. 254.

14. "Playwright's Moral Exercise," p. 1.

15. Review by Michael Walsh, July 17, 1958, p. 5.

16. Unsigned review in the *London Times,* July 17, 1958, p. 4.

17. Review by J. C. Trewin, August 2, 1958, p. 200.

18. Review by Eric Keown, July 23, 1958, pp. 118 - 19.

19. Review by Alan Brien, July 25, 1958, pp. 133 - 34.

20. Signed "Reuter," December 4, 1959, p. 15.

21. Review by Brooks Atkinson, December 3, 1959; *NYTCR,* 1959, p. 210.

22. John McClain; see note 10.

23. See, for example, John Russell Taylor, p. 9; and Arnold P. Hinchliffe, *British Theatre 1950 - 70* (Totowa, NJ, 1974), chapter four, entitled "1956 Annus Mirabilis."

24. Taylor believes that Shaffer used the same method in *Five Finger Exercise* that Ionesco used in *La Cantatrice chauve* (The Bald Prima Donna), that of stripping bare the characters and their way of life, p. 274.

Chapter Three

1. Peter Shaffer, *The Private Ear [and] The Public Eye* (New York, 1964), p. 22.
2. Review in the *Daily Telegraph*, May 11, 1962, p. 16.
3. Review in *Cue*, October 19, 1963, p. 28.
4. "Broadway in Review," *Educational Theatre Journal* 15 (1963), pp. 358 - 65.
5. Review in the *Illustrated London News*, May 26, 1962, p. 860.
6. Review in the *Evening Standard*, May 11, 1962, p. 21.
7. Review in the *New York Daily News*, October 10, 1963; *NYTCR*, 1963, p. 249.
8. Review in the *Christian Science Monitor*, May 12, 1962, p. 4.
9. Review in the *Daily Express*, May 12, 1962, p. 7.
10. Peter Shaffer, *Black Comedy [including] White Lies* (New York, 1967), p. 52.
11. At this point, Brindsley places the raincoat over the Wedgewood bowl; later, however, it is the porcelain Buddha which breaks.
12. For a discussion of the identification between Sophie and Tom, see Jules Glenn, "Anthony and Peter Shaffer's Plays: The Influence of Twinship on Creativity," *American Imago* 31 (1974), pp. 270 - 92.
13. Peter Shaffer, *The White Liars [and] Black Comedy* (New York, 1968), p. 3.
14. Mel Gussow in *Newsweek*, February 20, 1967, pp. 102 - 103; also Walter Kerr in the *New York Times*, February 13, 1967; *NYTCR*, 1967, pp. 373 - 74.
15. Unsigned review in *Time*, February 17, 1967, p. 70; and Walter Kerr in the *New York Times*, February 13, 1967, p. 42.

Chapter Four

1. Peter Shaffer, *The Royal Hunt of the Sun* (New York, 1964), p. v.
2. I am using the spelling of the names as they appear in the play and not as they appear in history books.
3. See William H. Prescott, *History of the Conquest of Peru* (New York, [1847]). Another historian, Philip Ainsworth Means, relates that Atahuallpa's real friend among the Spaniards was Hernando De Soto; see *Fall of the Inca Empire and the Spanish Rule in Peru: 1530 - 1780* (New York, 1932), p. 35.
4. Marshall Cohen, "Theater 66," *Partisan Review* (Spring 1966), pp. 269 - 76. Bettina L. Knapp, *Antonin Artaud: Man of Vision* (New York, 1969), p. 202, reads: "Peter Schaffer's [sic] *The Royal Hunt of the Sun* is, in my opinion, a virtual transposition of Artaud's metaphysical drama *The Conquest of Mexico*."
5. In *La Nef*, 63/64 (March-April 1950), pp. 159 - 65.
6. October 27, 1965; *NYTCR*, 1965, p. 294.

7. Review by Henry Hewes, November 13, 1965, p. 71.

8. Review by Theophilus Lewis, *America* 113 (November 20, 1965), pp. 648 - 49.

9. Review by John Chapman, October 27, 1965; *NYTCR*, 1965, p. 296.

10. Review in *Plays and Players*, June 1969, p. 70.

11. Review in *Plays and Players*, February 1965, p. 34.

12. For example, Milton Shulman, *Evening Standard*, July 8, 1964, p. 4; Charles Marowitz, *Encore* (March - April 1965), pp. 44 - 45.

13. For example, John Simon, *Hudson Review*, 18 (Winter 1965 - 66), pp. 571 - 74; Howard Taubman, *New York Times*, November 14, 1965, section two, p. 1.

14. John Russell Taylor, p. 277.

15. Robert Brustein, *The Third Theatre* (New York, 1969), p. 109.

16. Malcolm Rutherford, *Spectator* (July 17, 1964), pp. 82, 84.

17. Article in *New York Times*, November 14, 1965, section two, p. 1.

18. (Garden City, NY, 1970).

19. "To See the Soul of a Man . . . *[sic]*," *New York Times*, October 24, 1965, section two, p. 3.

20. "In Search of a God," *Plays and Players*, October 1964, p. 22.

Chapter Five

1. For B. A. Young (*Financial Times*, February 6, 1970, p. 3) the play is just not believable. Milton Shulman (*Evening Standard*, February 6, 1970, p. 24) saw in the play the archetypal Thinker and Artist rather than people. He found the play to be an interesting literary exercise, with flashes of profundity, poetry, and wit. There is no lack of intelligence in the work for Eric Shorter (*Daily Telegraph*, February 6, 1970, p. 16); Philip Hope-Wallace (*Guardian*, February 6, 1970, p. 8); or Jeremy Kingston (*Punch*, February 11, 1970, p. 236).

2. From the plays *Shrivings* and *Equus* by Peter Shaffer. Copyright 1974 by Peter Shaffer. Reprinted by permission of Atheneum Publishers. From 4th printing (New York, 1976), p. 135.

Chapter Six

1. For a psychiatrist's comments on this detail as well as on the twinship between Alan and Dysart, see Jules Glenn's "Anthony and Peter Shaffer's Plays: The Influence of Twinship on Creativity"; see Chapter 3, note 12.

2. I am referring here to De Nizza's speech in which he criticizes the Inca society for depriving its citizens of unhappiness, want, and inequality. Similarly, Dysart is reluctant to alleviate Alan's pain because it is: "His pain. His own. He made it . . . to go through life and call it yours—*your life*—you first have to get your own pain. Pain that's unique to you. You can't just dip into the common bin and say 'That's enough!' . . . He's done that" (p. 80).

3. I am indebted to Dr. Susan Robbins of the University of South Dakota for bringing her linguistic talents to this passage.

4. Sexual and religious fervor have always been two sides of the same coin. Witness, for example, Bernini's statue of St. Teresa, for which the artist is said to have used the expression of a woman during orgasm to capture the rapture of direct communication with God.

5. I appreciate the help of Dr. Brent Froberg, a Greek professor, for translating *dys* accurately for me.

6. See R. D. Laing, *The Politics of Experience* (New York, 1967), for a full treatment of this subject.

7. The Holy Bible (New York, 1901). All biblical quotations are from this edition.

8. See Richard Lewinsohn, *Animals, Men and Myths* (New York, 1954), p. 85.

9. George Gaylord Simpson, *Horses: The Story of the Horse Family in the Modern World and through Sixty Million Years of History* (New York, 1951), p. 30.

10. In *The Classical Journal* 65 (1970), p. 245.

11. "High Horse," in *Guardian*, August 8, 1973, p. 8.

12. D. H. Lawrence, *Mornings in Mexico [and] Etruscan Places*, 2nd ed. (London, 1965), p. 68.

13. D. H. Lawrence, "The Rocking-Horse Winner," in *The Complete Short Stories*, Vol. III (New York, 1962), p. 794.

14. See Rafael Martínez Nadal, *"El público." Amor: teatro y caballos en la obra de Federico García Lorca* (Oxford, England, 1970); also the English version *Lorca's "The Public": A Study of His Unfinished Play "El Público" and of Love and Death in the Work of Federico García Lorca* (London, 1974); Julian Palley, "Archetypal Symbols in *Bodas de Sangre*," *Hispania* 50 (1967), pp. 74 - 79; and Juan Villegas, "El leitmotif del caballo en *Bodas de sangre*," *Hispanófila* 29 (1967), pp. 21 - 36.

15. Federico García Lorca, *Obras completas*, 15th ed. (Madrid, 1969), p. 905. All references to García Lorca's work are from this edition.

16. All translations are my own and are free.

17. I thank Dr. Larry Vonalt of the University of Missouri-Rolla for this insight.

18. See. W. L. Warren, *King John* (New York, 1961), p. 81.

19. In *El mono piadoso y seis piezas de café-teatro* (Madrid, 1969), p. 63.

20. See note 11.

21. Aristotle, *Rhetoric [and] Poetics*, trans. by Rhys Roberts and Ingram Bywater, respectively (New York), 1954, p. 230.

22. During an interview at the playwright's New York penthouse, on January 6, 1978, Mr. Shaffer emphasized that first and foremost a dramatist must tell a story that will keep the attention of the audience.

23. Samuel Terrier, *"Equus:* Human Conflicts and the Trinity," *Christian Century* (May 18, 1977), pp. 472 - 76.

24. Martin Gottfried in *New York Post,* October 25, 1975; *NYTCR,* 1974, p. 206; and Walter Kerr in *New York Times,* October 5, 1975, section two, pp. 1, 5.

25. John Simon, "Hippodrama at the Psychodrome," *Hudson Review* 28 (Spring 1975), pp. 97 - 106.

26. Martin Gottfried in *New York Post,* February 24, 1977, p. 18.

27. Howard Kissel in *Women's Wear Daily,* October 18, 1974; *NYTCR,* 1974, pp. 203 - 204.

28. Edwin Wilson in *Wall Street Journal,* October 28, 1974; *NYTCR,* 1974, p. 203.

29. Review by Walter Kerr, November 3, 1974, section two, p. 1.

30. Review by Douglas Watt, October 25, 1974; *NYTCR,* 1974, pp. 201 - 202.

31. John Leonard in *New York Times,* May 26, 1976, p. 24; John Simon in *New York* magazine, November 11, 1974, p. 118.

32. Blurb that appeared frequently, as on May 31, 1976, p. 4.

33. See my bibliography for three of his articles.

34. "Psychoanalyst Says Nay to *Equus,*" *New York Times,* December 15, 1974, section two, p. 1.

Chapter Seven

1. Recall Pizarro's warning to Young Martin: "You trust me, I'll hurt you past believing," in his speech on pp. 17 - 18 of *The Royal Hunt of the Sun.*

2. In *Shrivings,* David smashes the death apple in an attempt to stop "the voice."

3. See John Hemming, *The Conquest of the Incas* (New York, 1970), pp. 34 - 35.

4. Shaffer conceived the idea for *The Public Eye* while he was at a rehearsal of *The Private Ear.*

5. In correspondence that I received from Mr Shaffer; postmarked May 3, 1976.

Selected Bibliography

Most of Shaffer's works are available in various editions. Only the editions used in this study are listed here.

PRIMARY SOURCES

1. Plays

Black Comedy [including] White Lies; Two Plays. New York: Stein and Day, 1967.

Equus [and] Shrivings; Two Plays, 4th printing. New York: Atheneum, 1976.

Five Finger Exercise; A Play. London: Samuel French, 1958.

The Private Ear [and] The Public Eye; Two Plays. New York: Stein and Day, 1964.

The Royal Hunt of the Sun; A Play Concerning the Conquest of Peru. New York: Stein and Day, 1964.

The White Liars [and] Black Comedy; Two One-Act Plays. New York: Samuel French, 1968.

2. Novels

How Doth the Little Crocodile?, with Anthony Shaffer. New York: Macmillan, 1957.

Withered Murder, with Anthony Shaffer. New York: Macmillan, 1956.

The Woman in the Wardrobe; A Light-Hearted Detective Story. Drawings by Nicolas Bentley. London: Evans Brothers, 1951.

3. Unpublished Radio and Television Scripts

"The Prodigal Father," aired on BBC radio, September 14, 1957.

"The Salt Land," produced by ITV, November 8, 1955.

4. Miscellaneous

FROST, DAVID, and NED SHERRIN. *That Was the Week That Was.* London: W. H. Allen, 1963. Contains two sketches by Peter Shaffer.

SECONDARY SOURCES

1. Books

ARISTOTLE. *Rhetoric [and] Poetics.* Trans. by Rhys Roberts and Ingram Bywater, respectively. New York: The Modern Library, 1954.

BROWN, JOHN RUSSELL, ed. *Modern British Dramatists: A Collection of*

Critical Essays. Englewood Cliffs, NJ: Prentice-Hall, 1968. Essays on British playwrights, none of whom is Peter Shaffer.

BRUSTEIN, ROBERT. *The Theatre of Revolt: An Approach to Modern Drama.* Boston and Toronto: Little, Brown and Co., 1974. International in its scope and informative in its contents, but the work stops short of mentioning Shaffer.

———. *The Third Theatre.* New York: Alfred A. Knopf, 1969. Contains an essay entitled "Peru in New York: *The Royal Hunt of the Sun* by Peter Shaffer."

BURGESS, ANTHONY. *A Clockwork Orange.* Afterword and glossary by Stanley Edgar Hyman. New York: W. W. Norton and Co., 1963. A novelistic treatment of the question of society's right to cure antisocial behavior. Worthwhile background reading for *Equus.*

CAVENDISH, RICHARD, ed. *Man, Myth and Magic: An Illustrated Encyclopedia of the Supernatural.* New York: Marshall Cavendish Corp., 1970. Volume ten has a section on horses and their symbolic value.

CHIARI, J. *Landmarks of Contemporary Drama.* London: Herbert Jenkins, 1965. Praise for *Five Finger Exercise* and disdain for *The Royal Hunt of the Sun,* in the chapter of "Concluding Remarks."

CIRLOT, J. E. *A Dictionary of Symbols,* 2nd ed. Trans. by Jack Sage. New York: Philosophical Library, Inc., 1971. A standard reference work on literary symbols, such as the horse.

COHN, RUBY. *Currents in Contemporary Drama.* Bloomington, IN, and London: Indiana University Press, 1969. A commentary on Shaffer in the context of modern British drama and a comment on *The Royal Hunt of the Sun.*

Contemporary Authors: A Bio-Bibliographical Guide to Current Authors and Their Work, revised ed. Ed. by Christine Nasso. Detroit: Gale Research Co., 1977. A chronology with criticism on some of Shaffer's plays appears in volume 25 - 28.

ELSON, JOHN. *Post-War British Theatre.* London, Henley-on-Thames, and Boston: Routledge and Kegan Paul, 1976. Comments on Shaffer's major plays, as well as comparisons between Shaffer's work and that of his contemporaries.

ESSLIN, MARTIN. *Reflections: Essays on Modern Theatre.* Garden City, NY: Doubleday and Co., 1969. The chapter "Brecht and the English Theatre" mentions *The Royal Hunt of the Sun.*

———. *The Theatre of the Absurd.* Garden City, NY: Doubleday and Co., 1969. Esslin does not mention Shaffer, who is not an Absurdist writer, but he does consider contemporaries of Shaffer, such as Osborne, Arden, and Pinter.

GARCÍA LORCA, FEDERICO, *Obras completas,* 15th ed. Madrid: Aguilar, 1969.

GASCOIGNE, BAMBER. *Twentieth Century Drama.* London: Hutchinson University Library, 1962. Does not treat the works of Shaffer, but does treat those of Osborne, Wesker, Behan, Delaney, Pinter, Whiting, and Bolt.

GASSNER, JOHN, and EDWARD QUINN, eds. *The Reader's Encyclopedia of World Drama.* New York: Thomas Y. Crowell Co., 1969. Notes on Shaffer's life and plays, through *Black Comedy.*

GILLIATT, PENELOPE. *Unholy Fools. Wits, Comics, Disturbers of Peace: Film and Theater.* New York: The Viking Press, 1973. One of the many articles is on the production of *Black Comedy* in Chichester.

GRAU, JACINTO. *Teatro,* 2nd ed. Buenos Aires: Losada, 1960. The theme and protagonist of *Las gafas de don Telesforo o un loco de buen capricho* parallel those of *The Public Eye.*

GREENE, NAOMI. *Antonin Artaud: Poet Without Words.* New York: Simon and Schuster, 1970. A discussion of *La Conquête du Mexique,* which some critics think influenced *The Royal Hunt of the Sun.*

HEMMING, JOHN. *The Conquest of the Incas.* New York: Harcourt Brace Jovanovich, 1970. Contains background information which is useful for appreciating *The Royal Hunt of the Sun* as historical drama.

HINCHLIFFE, ARNOLD P. *British Theatre, 1950 - 70.* Totowa, NJ: Rowman and Littlefield, 1974. Space does not permit the critic to "explain why the Shaffer brothers were so successful in the West End . . ." (p. 149), in this book, which contains valuable background information on the British theater.

THE HOLY BIBLE; Containing the Old and New Testaments. New York: Nelson and Sons, 1901.

HOMER. *Complete Works. The Iliad.* Trans. by Andrew Lang, Walter Leaf, and Ernest Myers. *The Odyssey.* Trans. by S. H. Butcher and Andrew Lang. New York: The Modern Library, 1950.

JUNG, C. G. *The Archetypes and the Collective Unconscious,* 2nd ed. Trans. by R. F. C. Hull. Princeton, NJ: Princeton University Press, 1975. A reference work on archetypal symbols.

————. *The Portable Jung.* Ed. and intro. by Joseph Campbell. Trans. by R. F. C. Hull. New York: The Viking Press, 1972. Contains ideas applicable to an appreciation of Shaffer's plays.

KERNODLE, GEORGE R. *Invitation to the Theatre.* New York: Harcourt, Brace and World, 1967. Commentaries on *The Royal Hunt of the Sun* as epic theater and on the film version (which Shaffer did not write) of *Five Finger Exercise.*

KNAPP, BETTINA L. *Antonin Artaud: Man of Vision.* New York: David Lewis, 1969. In this critic's view, *The Royal Hunt of the Sun* is a "virtual transposition" of *La Conquête du Mexique.*

LAING, R. D. *The Politics of Experience.* New York: Pantheon Books, 1967. A psychiatrist's thinking on who should and should not be cured of his individualizing personality traits.

LAMBERT, J. W. *Drama in Britain 1964 - 1973.* Harlow, Essex: Longman Group, 1974. Background reading on such institutions as the National Theatre.

LAWRENCE, D. H. *The Complete Short Stories*. Vol. III, 2nd ed. New York: The Viking Press, 1962. Contains "The Rocking-Horse Winner."

————. *Mornings in Mexico [and] Etruscan Places*. 2nd ed. Intro. by Richard Aldington. London: Heinemann, 1965.

LEWIS, ALLAN. *American Plays and Playwrights of the Contemporary Theatre*. New York: Crown Publishers, 1965. Although the plays are not American, Lewis mentions briefly *The Private Ear* and *The Public Eye*.

LEWINSOHN, RICHARD. *Animals, Men and Myths*. New York: Harper and Brothers, 1954. Trans. from the German. The role of horses in the classical Greek world.

LUMLEY, FREDERICK. *New Trends in Twentieth Century Drama: A Survey since Ibsen and Shaw*. New York: Oxford University Press, 1967. The brief section on Shaffer contains comments on *Five Finger Exercise, The Royal Hunt of the Sun, The Public Eye,* and *Black Comedy*.

MAROWITZ, CHARLES. *Confessions of a Counterfeit Critic: A London Theatre Notebook 1958 - 1971*. London: Eyre Methuen, 1973. Contains a reprint of his review from *Encore* on *The Royal Hunt of the Sun*.

MASCHLER, TOM, ed. *New English Dramatists*. Vol. IV. Harmondsworth, England: Penguin Books, [1962]. Includes the text of *Five Finger Exercise* and introductory comments on the play.

McGraw Hill Encyclopedia of World Drama. New York, 1972. Mention of Shaffer's plays through 1970, a paragraph each on *Five Finger Exercise* and *The Royal Hunt of the Sun*, as well as a biographical sketch of the playwright.

MEANS, PHILIP AINSWORTH. *Fall of the Inca Empire and the Spanish Rule in Peru: 1530 - 1780*. New York and London: Charles Scribner's Sons, 1932. Background reading for the historical events on which *The Royal Hunt of the Sun* is based.

PARKER, JOHN, original compiler. *Who's Who in the Theatre: A Biographical Record of the Contemporary Stage,* 15th ed. London: Pitman and Sons, 1972. A one-paragraph biographical and professional résumé through 1970.

PRESCOTT, WILLIAM H. *History of the Conquest of Peru*. Two vols. New York: Fred De Fau and Co., [1847]. Shaffer's source for *The Royal Hunt of the Sun*.

RICHARD, STANLEY, ed. *Best Plays of the Sixties*. Garden City, NY: Doubleday and Co., 1970. Includes *The Royal Hunt of the Sun*, as well as a biographical sketch.

ROY, EMIL. *British Drama since Shaw*. Carbondale and Edwardsville, IL: Southern Illinois University Press; and London and Amsterdam: Feller and Simons, 1972. Only the briefest mention of Shaffer on the last page of the book.

RUIBAL, JOSÉ. "Los ojos" in *El mono piadoso y seis piezas de café-teatro*. Madrid: Escelicer, 1969. Eyes in a Spanish play.

SALEM, DANIEL. *La Révolution théâtrale actuelle en Angleterre.* Paris: Denoël, 1969. Cursory remarks on *Five Finger Exercise, The Royal Hunt of the Sun, Black Comedy,* and on Shaffer the man.

STYAN, J. L. *The Dark Comedy: The Development of Modern Comic Tragedy.* Cambridge, England: Cambridge University Press, 1962. Styan enumerates and comments on the essential elements of dark comedy.

TAYLOR, JOHN RUSSELL. *Anger and After: A Guide to the New British Drama.* London: Methuen and Co., 1962 and 1969; *The Angry Theatre: New British Drama.* New York: Hill and Wang, 1969. All essentially the same work, but the two 1969 editions mention *The Public Eye, The Private Ear, Black Comedy,* and *The White Liars* while the 1962 edition does not.

————. *Peter Shaffer.* Ed. by Ian Scott-Kilvert. No. 244 of the Writers and Their Work series. Harlow, Essex: Longman House, 1974. An essay on the plays from *Five Finger Exercise* through *Equus.*

————. *The Rise and Fall of the Well-Made Play.* New York: Hill and Wang, 1967. The most casual comment in the last chapter on *Five Finger Exercise.*

VINSON, JAMES, ed. *Contemporary Dramatists.* Preface by Ruby Cohn. New York: St. Martin's Press; and London: St. James Press, 1973. John Elsom prepared the biographical sketch, bibliography, and notes on Shaffer's works.

WAKEMAN, JOHN, ed. *World Authors 1950 - 1970.* New York: H. W. Wilson Co., 1975. Biographical sketch and commentary on the plays.

WELLWARTH, GEORGE. *The Theater of Protest and Paradox: Developments in the Avant-Garde Drama.* New York: New York University Press, 1964. Wellwarth's inclusion of Shaffer is limited to the comment that *Five Finger Exercise* is an example of a play in which a dramatist tries to exorcise his middle-class background by denigrating it.

˙2. Articles

ARTAUD, ANTONIN. "La Conquête du Mexique," *La Nef* 63/64 (March - April 1950), pp. 159 - 65. An outline of the play which some critics believe that Shaffer used as a model for *The Royal Hunt of the Sun.*

BUCKLEY, TOM. " 'Write Me' Said the Play to Peter Shaffer." *New York Times Magazine,* April 13, 1975, pp. 20 - 21, 25 - 26, 28, 30, 32, 34, 37 - 38, 40. Shaffer reveals details of the actual case that inspired *Equus* and talks about his play.

GIANAKARIS, C. J. "The Theatre of the Mind in Miller, Osborne and Shaffer." *Renascence* 30, i (Autumn 1977), pp. 33 - 42. Some new insights on *Equus.*

GLENN, JULES. "Anthony and Peter Shaffer's Plays: The Influence of Twinship on Creativity." *American Imago* 31 (1974), pp. 270 - 92. Dr. Glenn, a psychiatrist, demonstrates how the two main characters in many of Shaffer's plays are "doubles" and exhibit the characteristics typical of twins.

———. "Twins in Disguise: A Psychoanalytic Essay on *Sleuth* and *The Royal Hunt of the Sun.*" *Psychoanalytic Quarterly* 43, ii, (1974), pp. 288 - 302. A study of the close kinship between the protagonists in the two plays and of their twin traits.

———. "Twins in Disguise. II. Content, Form and Style in Plays by Anthony and Peter Shaffer." *The International Review of Psycho-Analysis* 1, iii (1974), pp. 373 - 81. Dr. Glenn explores further the twin elements in *Sleuth*, as well as in Anthony's *Frenzy* and Peter's *Black Comedy, The White Liars, White Lies,* and *The Public Eye.*

HAYMAN, RONALD. "Like a Woman They Keep Going Back To." *Drama* (Autumn 1970), pp. 57 - 64. On selected, post-1956, British Playwrights. The remarks on Shaffer are more general than profound.

JONES, JULIAN WARD, JR. "The Trojan Horse, *Timeo Danaos et dona ferentis.*" *Classical Journal* 65, vi (1970), pp. 241 - 47. Sheds light on the religious consideration of equine imagery.

PENNEL, CHARLES A. "The Plays of Peter Shaffer: Experiment in Convention." *Kansas Quarterly* 3, ii (1971), pp. 100 - 109. A pioneer article on Shaffer's theater, *Five Finger Exercise* through *The Battle of Shrivings.*

"Philip Oaks Talks to Peter Shaffer." *London Sunday Times,* July 29, 1973, p. 33. An interview with Shaffer about his work and the theater in general.

ROGOFF, GORDON. "Richard's Himself Again: Journey to an Actor's Theatre." *Tulane Drama Review* (Winter 1966), pp. 29 - 40. Rogoff on the work of the National Theatre.

SHAFFER, PETER. "In Search of a God." *Plays and Players* (October 1964), p. 22. Shaffer on *The Royal Hunt of the Sun.*

———. "Labels Aren't for Playwrights." *Theatre Arts* (February 1960), pp. 20 - 21. An early interview, in which Shaffer reveals that he wants to write in a variety of styles.

SIMON, JOHN. "Hippodrama at the Psychodrome." *Hudson Review* 28 (Spring 1975), pp. 97 - 106. An unwarrantedly severe critique of *Equus*, as well as an attempt to prove that it is somehow a defense of homosexuality, and a dishonest one at that.

STACY, JAMES R. "The Sun and the Horse: Peter Shaffer's Search for Worship." *Educational Theatre Journal* 28, iii (1976), pp. 325 - 35. Not Shaffer's, as the title suggests, but rather the fictional Pizarro's and Alan Strang's search for worship.

TERRIER, SAMUEL. "*Equus:* Human Conflicts and the Trinity." *Christian Century* (May 18, 1977), pp. 472 - 76. A Christian approach to *Equus.*

TOBIAS, TOBI. "Playing without Words." *Dance Magazine* (May 1975), pp. 48 - 50. Primarily concerned with the role of the horse-actors in *Equus.*

VANDENBROUCKE, RUSSELL. "*Equus:* Modern Myth in the Making." *Drama and Theatre* 12 (1975), pp. 129 - 33. The title is impressive; the article consists mostly of plot summary.

3. A Doctoral Dissertation

LAWSON, WAYNE PAUL. "The Dramatic Hunt: A Critical Evaluation of Peter Shaffer's Plays." Ph.D. dissertation, written at The Ohio State University, 1973. Lawson places Shaffer within the context of British drama and analyzes the plays from *Five Finger Exercise* through *The Battle of Shrivings*.

Index

162